SHEPHERD'S NOTES

SHEPHERD'S NOTES

When you need a guide through the Scriptures

Psalms 101-150

BROADMAN
&HOLMAN
PUBLISHERS

Nashville, Tennessee

Shepherd's Notes®—*Psalms 101–150*
© 1999
by Broadman & Holman Publishers
Nashville, Tennessee
All rights reserved
Printed in the United States of America

0–8054–9341–7
Dewey Decimal Classification: 223.20
Subject Heading: BIBLE. O.T. PSALMS
Library of Congress Card Catalog Number: 99–11545

Library of Congress Cataloging-in-Publication Data
Gould, Dana, 1951–
Psalms 101–150 / Dana Gould, editor [i.e. author].
    p. cm. — (Shepherd's notes)
  Includes bibliographical references.
  ISBN 0–8054–9341–7
    1. Bible. O.T. Psalms—Study and teaching.   I. Title.   II. Title: Psalms one hundred one through one hundred fifty.   III. Title: Psalms one hundred and one through one hundred fifty. IV. Series
  BS1451.G68   1999
  223'.207—dc21
        99–11545
        CIP

1 2 3 4 5   03 02 01 00 99

CONTENTS

FOREWORD

Dear Reader:

Shepherd's Notes are designed to give you a quick, step-by-step overview of every book of the Bible. They are not meant to be substitutes for the biblical text; rather, they are study guides intended to help you explore the wisdom of Scripture in personal or group study and to apply that wisdom successfully in your own life.

Shepherd's Notes guide you through the main themes of each book of the Bible and illuminate fascinating details through appropriate commentary and reference notes. Historical and cultural background information brings the Bible into sharper focus.

Six different icons, used throughout the series, call your attention to historical-cultural information, Old Testament and New Testament references, word pictures, unit summaries, and personal application for everyday life.

Whether you are a novice or a veteran at Bible study, I believe you will find *Shepherd's Notes* a resource that will take you to a new level in your mining and applying the riches of Scripture.

In Him,

David R. Shepherd
Editor-in-Chief

DESIGNED FOR THE BUSY USER

Shepherd's Notes for Psalms 101–150 is designed to provide an easy-to-use tool for getting a quick handle on this portion of this significant Bible book's important features, and for gaining an understanding of their messages. Information available in more difficult-to-use reference works has been incorporated into the *Shepherd's Notes* format. This brings you the benefits of many advanced and expensive works packed into one small volume.

Shepherd's Notes are for laymen, pastors, teachers, small-group leaders and participants, as well as the classroom student. Enrich your personal study or quiet time. Shorten your class or small-group preparation time as you gain valuable insights into the truths of God's Word that you can pass along to your students or group members.

DESIGNED FOR QUICK ACCESS

Bible students with time constraints will especially appreciate the timesaving features built into the *Shepherd's Notes*. All features are intended to aid a quick and concise encounter with the heart of the messages of Psalms 101–150.

Concise Commentary. Short sections provide quick "snapshots" of the themes of the psalms.

Outlined Text. Comprehensive outlines cover the entire text of Psalms 101–150. This is a valuable feature for following each psalm's flow, allowing for a quick, easy way to locate a particular passage.

Shepherd's Notes. These summary statements or capsule thoughts appear at the close of every key section of the Psalms. While functioning in part as a quick summary, they also deliver the essence of the the psalm.

Icons. Various icons in the margin highlight recurring themes in Psalms 101–150, aiding in selective searching or tracing of those themes.

Questions to Guide Your Study. These thought-provoking questions and discussion starters are designed to encourage interaction with the truth and principles of God's Word.

DESIGNED TO WORK FOR YOU

Personal Study. Using the *Shepherd's Notes* with a passage of Scripture can enlighten your study and take it to a new level. At your fingertips is information that would require searching several volumes to find. In addition, many points of application occur throughout the volume, contributing to personal growth.

Teaching. Outlines frame the text of Psalms 101–150, providing a logical presentation of their messages. Capsule thoughts designated as "Shepherd's Notes" provide summary statements for presenting the essence of key points and events. Application icons point out personal application of the messages of the psalms. Historical Context icons indicate where cultural and historical background information is supplied.

Group Study. Shepherd's Notes can be an excellent companion volume to use for gaining a quick but accurate understanding of the messages of Psalms 101–150. Each group member can benefit from having his or her own copy. The *Note's* format accommodates the study of themes throughout Psalms 101–150. Leaders may use its flexible features to prepare for group sessions or use them during group sessions. Questions to guide your study can spark discussion of Psalms 101–150's key points and truths to be discovered in these profound psalms.

LIST OF MARGIN ICONS USED IN PSALMS 101–150

Shepherd's Notes. Placed at the end of each section, a capsule statement provides the reader with the essence of the message of that section.

Historical Context. To indicate historical information—historical, biographical, cultural—and provide insight on the understanding or interpretation of a passage.

Old Testament Reference. Used when the writer refers to Old Testament passages or when Old Testament passages illuminate a text.

New Testament Reference. Used when the writer refers to New Testament passages that are either fulfilled prophecy, an antitype of an Old Testament type, or a New Testament text which in some other way illuminates the passages under discussion.

Personal Application. Used when the text provides a personal or universal application of truth.

Word Picture. Indicates that the meaning of a specific word or phrase is illustrated so as to shed light on it.

INTRODUCTION

The book of Psalms or the *Psalter* is the hymnal of Israelite worship and the Bible's book of personal devotions. In it we not only find expression of all the emotions of life but also some of the most profound teaching in the entire Bible.

DATE AND AUTHORSHIP OF THE PSALMS

The Psalter was not completed until late in Israelite history (in the postexilic era). But it contains hymns written over a period of hundreds of years.

Evidence of the superscriptions. A primary source of information regarding the date and authorship of individual psalms are the superscriptions found above many psalms. According to these, some of the authors include David, the sons of Korah, Asaph, Moses, and Solomon. Other psalms, including some of the "Psalms of Ascent" (Pss. 120–134) and "Hallelujah" psalms (Pss. 146–150) are anonymous. These superscriptions, if taken at face value, would date many of the psalms to the early tenth century (psalms of David) and at least one to the fifteenth century (Ps. 90).

Meaning and reliability of the superscriptions. Some scholars, however, question whether the superscriptions are meant to ascribe authorship to the Psalms. A more serious question is whether the superscriptions are reliable. Some scholars believe they were added at a late date and are no more than conjectures that have no real historical value. But there are good reasons to believe the superscriptions can be trusted.

The phrase *ledawid* used frequently in the psalm superscriptions could mean "by David" or "for David." But the clause following the superscription to Psalm 18 favors "by David."

Many of the psalm superscriptions refer to incidents in the life of David about which Samuel and Chronicles say nothing. For example, the superscription of Psalm 60 mentions battles with Aram-Naharaim, Aram-Zobah, and Edom. It would be strange if, in the late postexilic period, rabbis invented this. Another example is the superscription of Psalm 7, which speaks of a certain "Cush the Benjamite" (he is mentioned only here in the Old Testament). If the superscriptions were late fabrications, one would expect that they would refer more to incidents from David's life mentioned in Samuel.

Many of the psalm superscriptions contain technical musical terms, the meanings of which were already lost by the time the Old Testament was translated into Greek. For example, *lammenasseah*, the word which means "for the choir leader," is wrongly translated "to the end" in the Septuagint, the pre-Christian Greek translation of the Old Testament. A number of these terms are still not understood.

Obscure or difficult words in the superscriptions include:

- *Song Titles:* "Do Not Destroy"; "A Dove on Distant Oaks"; "The Doe of the Morning"; "Lilies"; "The Lilies of the Covenant"; and "Mahalath"
- *Musical Instruments* or *Technical Terms:* "stringed instruments" and "Sheminith"
- *Musical Guilds* or *Singers:* "Asaph"; "Sons of Korah"; "Heman the Ezrahite"; "Ethan the Ezrahite"
- *Types of Psalms:* "Songs of Ascent," likely sung by those who were making a pilgrimage to Jerusalem; *maskil,* possibly an instructional or meditative psalm.

Ancient terminology and references to old guilds and bygone events all imply that the titles are very old. This supports confidence in their reliability.

Davidic authorship of Psalms. Many scholars have asserted that David did not write the Psalms attributed to him. But there are no historical reasons why David could not have authored those Psalms. David had a reputation as a singer and as a devoted servant of the Lord, and nothing in his life is incompatible with his being a psalmist.

One difficulty that has been raised is that some of the Psalms of David seem to refer to the Temple (for example, 27:4), which did not exist in his day. But terms like "house of the Lord," "holy place," and "house of God" are regularly used of the tent of meeting and need not be taken as references to Solomon's Temple (see Exod. 28:43; 29:30; Josh. 6:24).

Other psalms that mention the Temple, however, are also ascribed to David (Pss. 5; 11; 18; 27; 29; 65; 68; 138). The word *temple* (*hêkal*) does not necessarily refer to Solomon's Temple. The word *hêkal* is used in 1 Samuel 1:9; 3:3 of the tabernacle. It also refers sometimes to God's dwelling place as in 2 Samuel 22:7. In Psalm 27 God's house is called "house," "temple," "booth," and "tent."

The date of the Psalms. Earlier critics dated many of the Psalms late in Israel's history, some as late as the Maccabean period. For two reasons, however, this is no longer possible.

First, the Ugaritic songs and hymns show parallels to many of the Psalms. The grammar and poetic forms are similar. The Ugaritic tradition of hymn writing is ancient (before the twelfth

Ugarit was an important city in Syria whose excavation has provided tablets giving closest primary evidence available for reconstructing the Canaanite religion that was a perennial temptation to Israel.

century B.C.) and implies that many of the Psalms may be ancient too.

Second, a fragmentary, second-century B.C. copy of the biblical collection of Psalms was found in the Dead Sea Scrolls. This proves beyond doubt that the Psalms were composed well before the second century B.C., since it must have taken a long time for the written Psalms to be recognized as Scripture and for the Psalter to be organized.

There is no reason, therefore, to date all the Psalms late. Generally speaking, they can be dated to three broad periods: (1) *Preexilic.* This would include those Psalms that are very much like the Ugaritic songs, the royal psalms, and those that mention the Northern Kingdom. (2) *Exilic.* This would include the dirge songs that lament the fall of Jerusalem and call for vengeance on the Edomites and others. (3) *Early postexilic.* This would include Psalms that emphasize the written law, such as Psalm 119.

THE COMPILATION OF THE PSALMS

Psalms divides into five sections or "books":

Book One:	Psalms 1–41
Book Two:	Psalms 42–72
Book Three:	Psalms 73–89
Book Four:	Psalms 90–106
Book Five:	Psalms 107–150

We have no precise information regarding the dates when the five books of the Psalms were compiled or what the criteria of compilation were. Psalm 72:20 implies that a compilation of David's psalms was made shortly after his death.

In Hezekiah's time there were collections of the psalms of David and Asaph, which may account for the bulk of the first three books (2 Chron. 29:30). At a later date another scribe may have collected the remaining books of the Psalter. Psalms was put into its final form some time in the postexilic period.

The five books each close with a doxology, and Psalm 150 is a concluding doxology for the entire Psalter. But the numbering of the Psalms varies. The Jerusalem Talmud speaks of 147 psalms. The Septuagint divides Psalms 116 and 147 into two psalms each but numbers Psalms 9 and 10 and Psalms 114 and 115 as one psalm each.

King Hezekiah and his officials ordered the Levites to praise the Lord with the words of David and of Asaph the seer. So they sang praises with gladness and bowed their heads and worshiped (2 Chron. 29:30).

TYPES OF PSALMS

When studying a psalm, one should ask the following questions: (1) Was it sung by an individual or the congregation? (2) What was the psalm's purpose (praise, cry for help, thanksgiving, admonition)? (3) Does it mention any special themes, such as the royal house or Zion? By asking these questions, scholars have identified a number of psalm types.

Hymns. In this type of psalm, the whole congregation praises God for His works or attributes (Ps. 105). Six subcategories of hymns are:

Victory songs, which praise God for His victories over the nations (Ps. 68);

Processional hymns, sung as the worshipers moved into the temple area (Ps. 24);

Zion songs which praise God and specifically refer to His presence in Zion (Ps. 48);

Songs of the *Lord's reign,* which include the words, "The LORD reigns" (Ps. 99);

Antiphonal hymns chanted by either the priests or choir with the congregation responding antiphonally (Ps. 136); and

Hallelujah hymns, which begin or end with "Praise the LORD!" (Hebrew, *hallelu Yah;* Ps. 146).

Community complaints. In these psalms the whole nation voiced its complaints over problems it was facing, such as defeat in battle, famine, or drought (Ps. 74). A subcategory of this is the *national imprecation,* in which the people cursed their oppressors as enemies of Israel's God (Ps. 83).

Individual complaints. These psalms are like the community complaint except that they were prayers given by one person instead of the whole nation. The reason for the prayers might be that the individual was sick, hounded by enemies, or in need of confessing personal sin (Ps. 13). This type of psalm may include substantial *imprecation* or curses against the psalmist's personal enemies (Ps. 5). A subcategory is the *penitential psalm,* in which the speaker is dominated by a sense of guilt (Ps. 51).

Individual songs of thanksgiving. In these psalms an individual praises God for some saving act. Usually it alludes to a time that the individual was sick or in some other kind of trouble (Ps. 116).

Royal psalms. These psalms deal with the king and the royal house. Subcategories include:

Wedding songs, sung at the marriage of the king (Ps. 45);

Coronation songs (Ps. 72);

Prayers for victory, chanted when the king went to war (Ps. 20); and

Votive psalms, perhaps sung by the king at his coronation as a vow to be faithful and upright (Ps. 101).

Torah psalms. These psalms give moral or religious instruction (Pss. 1; 127). Subcategories include:

Testimony songs in which the psalmist used his personal experience of God's salvation to encourage the hearer (Ps. 32); and

Wisdom songs, in which the psalmist instructed the hearer more in practical wisdom similar to that in Proverbs than in the law (Ps. 49).

Oracle psalms. These psalms report a decree of God (Ps. 82). The content of the oracle is often divine judgment, and the psalm concludes with a prayer for God to carry out His decree. But see also Psalm 87, an oracle of salvation for the Gentiles.

Blessing psalms. In these psalms a priest pronounces a blessing upon the hearer(s) (Ps. 128).

Taunt songs. These psalms reproach the godless for their vile behavior and promise that their doom is near (Ps. 52).

Songs of trust. In these psalms the psalmist may face difficulty but remains assured of God's help and proclaims his faith and trust (Ps. 11).

When interpreting a psalm, it is important first to determine what kind of psalm it is. In this way one can see how the psalmist intended it to be read. (See article at the back of this book, "Types of Old Testament Literature.")

Torah is a Hebrew word normally translated "law" which eventually became a title for the Pentateuch, the first five books of the Old Testament.

THEOLOGICAL SIGNIFICANCE OF THE PSALMS

The Psalms help today's believers to understand God, themselves, and their relationship to God. The Psalms picture God as the Creator, who is worthy of praise and is capable of using His creative might to rescue His people from current distress. The Psalms picture God as the just Judge of all the world who rewards the righteous and opposes the wicked.

Prayers that God should curse the enemies of the psalmist must be understood in part as affirmations of God's justice and the certainty of His judgment. The Psalms picture God as the faithful friend of the oppressed. The Psalms offer a refresher course in God's faithfulness throughout Israel's history. The Psalms highlight God's promises to David and his descendants, promises that are not finally realized until Christ.

The Psalms picture the full range of human emotions: joy, despair, guilt, consolation, love, hate, thankfulness, and dissatisfaction. The Psalms thus remind us that all of life is under God's lordship. The Psalms likewise illustrate the broad range of human responses to God: praise, confession, pleas for help, thanksgiving. The Psalms thus serve as a sourcebook for Christian worship, both public and private.

THE FAITH OF THE PSALMS

As noted, the Psalms set forth the basic faith of the Hebrew people. God and man are the two basic focal points of that faith. These were the two inescapable realities. A religion which loses sight of either has failed to meet human needs. Their ancient faith also had two basic emphases: human need and divine providence. The Hebrew people were overwhelmingly aware

John Calvin called the Psalms "An Anatomy of Parts of the Soul." Calvin says, "There is not an emotion of which anyone can be conscious that is not here represented as in a mirror. Or, rather, the Holy Spirit has here drawn to the life all the griefs, sorrows, fears, doubts, hopes, cares, perplexities, in short, all the distracting emotions with which the minds of men are wont to be agitated." Calvin goes on to say that here we see God's servants laying open to God their inner thoughts and affections. The Psalms call us to lay before God all of our infirmities and vices.

that the plight of humanity was quite desperate as they faced the problems of sin, guilt, and evil. They were equally certain that God was sovereign, His purposes were good, and He would ultimately be victorious. The consequences of the divine sovereignty brought to the hearts and the lips of the Hebrews both praise and thanksgiving. They praised God for what He was and thanked Him for what He had done.

Finally, the faith of the psalmists can be characterized as having four dimensions. They always looked back to the past, to God's great acts of creation and more especially to His great acts of redemption and deliverance. In the present dimension of their faith, they were aware that God was with them, even when they did not "feel" His presence. Where they were, He was. Because of what God had done and because of their present experience with Him, they could look forward to being in His presence in the future. This gave them hope. The fourth dimension to the faith of the psalmists was timelessness. Their faith transcended time and speaks to the hearts of all people everywhere. This makes the book of Psalms a universal favorite among people. Wherever we are in our spiritual pilgrimage, we can find psalms which express our deepest thoughts, our greatest hopes, and our utmost certainties.

THE PSALMS FOR BELIEVERS TODAY

The list of teachings we gain from Psalms has no end. Its 150 songs call us to pray, to praise, to confess, and to testify. The prayer path to God is open at all times for all people in all situations. At all times we should take our feelings to God. He hears and accepts us. In His own way He answers. He brings salvation to our lives. Sin plagues each of us. We rebel against God's way.

God waits for us to confess our sins. He does not give us our deserts.

He forgives, redeems, and renews our lives. We may not be able to sing. We can praise God. We need to be aware of the great acts He is accomplishing in our lives and the great things He has accomplished for us in creation and in His saving actions through Jesus Christ. Knowing He acts for us, we can rejoice and praise Him at all times. We have no monopoly on God. He has chosen to help all nations praise Him. We must daily testify to others what God has done for us.

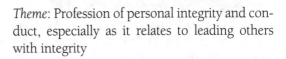

PSALM 101: WITH INTEGRITY OF HEART

Background: This psalm is the Davidic king's prayer and pledge. It holds up an ideal for all who serve in positions of authority in any age. Its focus is political ethics.

Theme: Profession of personal integrity and conduct, especially as it relates to leading others with integrity

Reader Insights: A votive psalm. This kind of psalm was perhaps sung by the king at his coronation as a vow to be faithful and upright.

PSALM SUMMARY

The ruler's integrity (101:1–4). The king promised to value loyalty and justice (v. 1). He determined to walk with integrity, "to lead a blameless life," not giving place to anything base in his personal life (vv. 2–3). He will keep himself from evil, reward the righteous, and root out evil and corruption in public life (vv. 4–5). The ruler's resolve shows that worship and ethics should be inseparable.

Ethics in public life (101:5–8). The king did not try to separate personal ethics from public life.

He vowed that he would not tolerate those who are slanderers, arrogant, deceitful, or liars. Such a promise could call for cleaning house in much of modern public service. A leader who has integrity will seek dependable persons to work with him.

- *The ruler determined to walk with integrity,*
- *not giving way to evil in his life. A leader*
- *who has integrity will seek dependable per-*
- *sons to work with him.*

GUIDING QUESTION
What are this psalm's implications for leaders today—religious and secular?

"Lead a blameless life"
The word *blameless* carries the root ideas of "completeness, integrity." A person who is blameless leads a life in "which no corruption or compromise is allowed to eat into it" (Derek Kidner, *Psalms 73–150* [Downers Grove: Inter-Varsity Press, 1975], 358).

Background: This psalm may have been written during the Jewish Exile in Babylon. It reflects both personal and corporate suffering.

Penitential Psalms

Penitential psalms are a subcategory of the individual lament. In these kinds of psalms, suffering is the occasion for searching one's heart before God.

Some suggest that Psalm 103 is a companion poem that answers the thought expressed in Psalm 102.

PSALM 102: IN TIMES OF TROUBLE

Theme: Seeking hope

Reader Insights: This is one of the individual laments called the "penitential" psalms (see Pss. 6; 32; 38; 51; 130; 143). It deals with the plight of the psalmist and the nation (illness and exile) in the light of God's eternal nature.

PSALM SUMMARY

The psalmist's illness and isolation (102:1–11). The psalmist pleaded with God to hear and answer his prayer for deliverance (vv. 1–2). He employed vivid pictures to describe his situation (vv. 3–7). Added to his illness and isolation was the ridicule of his enemies (v. 8). He had eaten ashes for bread and tears mixed with his drink (v. 9). He considered his suffering to be a punishment from God (vv. 10–11).

God will deliver and restore (102:12–22). The psalmist moved from personal to corporate concerns, appealing to God to "have compassion on Zion" (v. 13) and restore her. As a result, he wrote, "people not yet created [unborn] may praise the Lord" (v. 18). That promise was fulfilled. Generations of Jews have blessed the Lord for answering this prayer. God hears and delivers the oppressed (v. 20). People of all nations worship God in gratitude (v. 22).

Eternal God (102:23–28). The psalmist returned to the writing of his distress but saw it in the light of God's eternity. God outlives all generations (v. 24). He laid the foundation of the earth long ago. Heaven and earth will one day wear out like old clothes and be cast aside. But God goes on forever: "You remain the same" (v. 27). God has always existed and always will. In contrast, the world and mankind are transient.

Hebrews 1:10–12 quotes Psalm 102:25–27 from the Greek translation of the Old Testament, the Septuagint.

■ *The psalmist pleaded with God to hear and*
■ *answer his prayer for deliverance. He*
■ *described his predicament very graphically,*
■ *considering his suffering to be a punishment*
■ *from God. The psalmist declared God to be a*
■ *God of compassion. He hears and delivers*
■ *the oppressed. The psalmist compared his*
■ *distress to God's eternality. Although his suf-*
■ *fering would eventually end, God goes on*
■ *forever.*

GUIDING QUESTION

What benefit comes from comparing our transient, earthly existence with God's eternality?

PSALM 103: "PRAISE THE LORD"

Theme: Personal praise for God's blessings

Reader Insights: A hymn. The artful simplicity of this great psalm teaches that God knows mankind in its frailty and loves humanity still. It focuses on the brevity of human life and the eternal kingship of God. This hymn of praise has inspired many Christian hymns, including "Praise, My Soul, the King of Heaven."

PSALM SUMMARY

Personal praise (103:1–5). The psalmist called on his soul to praise the Lord. By *soul* he meant his whole being—intellect, emotions, and spirit—not just some part of his person. God's holy name means His revealed character (v. 1). The psalmist noted several of God's benefits, His actions on our behalf, one of which is renewing our youth like the eagle's (vv. 2–5).

National praise (103:6–18). The psalm next celebrated God's blessings on the nation. God provides justice for the oppressed (v. 6). He is also compassionate and merciful (vv. 7–8). His anger is not without limits, and He does not hold a grudge (v. 9). God punishes His people when they sin, but not as much as their iniquity deserves. His punishment is tempered (v. 10). His steadfast love is limitless (v. 11), and He forgives our sins (v. 12). God is a Father to His children, tender and understanding (vv. 13–14). He knows our frailty (vv. 15–16). Our weakness is a dramatic contrast to God's everlasting love (v. 17). He rewards those who "keep his covenant" (v. 18).

Praise from all creation (103:19–22). While God may dwell in the midst of His people, in the Temple, His throne is in the heavens (v. 19). He is king of heaven and earth. His kingdom is the universe. The psalmist called on the angels as well as on mankind to "Praise the LORD." Note that this phrase is repeated four times in poetic fashion in verses 20–22. The pattern of praise progresses from an individual to the congregation and the angels to the entire created order. Then the psalmist came back to his point of beginning. He concluded with the words, "Praise the LORD, O my soul."

- ■ *The psalmist called on his soul to bless God.*
- ■ *He noted several of God's actions on behalf of*
- ■ *His people. He announced that God is king of*
- ■ *heaven and earth. He called on all people to*
- ■ *praise God, concluding with the words,*
- ■ *"Praise the LORD, O my soul."*

GUIDING QUESTION

What was the psalmist's concept of the *soul*? What makes this an important biblical concept?

PSALM 104: GOD'S MIGHTY WORK IN CREATION

Theme: The greatness of God

Reader Insights: A hymn. This is a poem of sheer grandeur. It was the inspiration for the hymn: "O Worship the King." It is a colorful paraphrase of the creation story (Gen. 1) and is similar to Job 38–41.

PSALM SUMMARY

Beginning with the heavens (104:1–4). Both Psalms 103 and 104 end with praise: "Praise the LORD, O my soul." This section depicts God in His majesty and glory. He wears light as His mantle. He rides on the wings of the wind and rides the clouds as His chariot. The winds are His messengers; and the lightning bolts are His servants (v. 4).

Moving to the earth (104:5–30). The earth was created at God's word and is subject to His control. When He speaks, the chaotic waters of the deep flee to their proper place (vv. 7–9). The winds and waves obey Him (and His Son). Streams and rain provide essential water for vegetation and animal life (vv. 10–13). Grass and crops provide food for people and animals. Wine makes people glad; olive oil is their cosmetic; and bread makes them strong (v. 15). These were the principal crops in Palestine.

God provides trees for the birds (v. 17) and mountains for the wild goats and burrowing badgers (v. 18). The moon marks the seasons (v. 19). Nighttime is for the animals of prey (vv. 20–21) and daylight is for mankind's work (vv.

22–23). The sea is "vast and spacious," teeming with life, including Leviathan—probably the whale. Great ships sail on it (vv. 25–26).

God provides for His creatures (vv. 27–28). When He withholds His breath, they return to dust (v. 29). Yet His Spirit can create new life. (On the new creation, see Isaiah 65:17; 66:22; 2 Peter 3:13: Revelation 21:1.) Every living thing and person is dependent on God. He is the Author of life. It is His good gift to be received with gratitude.

A doxology (104:31–35). This is a lyrical prayer that God's glory will last forever.

- *This section depicts God in His majesty and*
- *glory. The first thing He created was light,*
- *also a symbol of His divine presence. The*
- *earth was created at God's word and it is*
- *subject to His sovereign control. Every living*
- *thing and person is dependent on God, and*
- *He provides for His creation. The psalmist*
- *closed the psalm with a doxology and a shout*
- *of praise: "Praise the LORD, O my soul!"*

GUIDING QUESTION

What was the psalmist's response to all that he contemplated? What is your response to this song of praise?

Background: This psalm gives an account of God's mighty acts in the history of the Israelites from the time of Abraham to their settling in the Promised Land. Psalm 105:1–15 are quoted in the account of King David's bringing the ark of the covenant to Jerusalem (1 Chron. 16).

PSALM 105: LORD OF HISTORY

Theme: The history of salvation

Reader Insights: A hallelujah hymn. The psalmist's purpose is to show how God had fulfilled His promise to Abraham and his descendants. The psalm invites those who read and hear it to "tell of all his wonderful acts" (v. 2) and to "keep his precepts" (v. 45).

PSALM SUMMARY

Remember God's works and sing praise (105:1–6). God's mighty acts and miracles on behalf of His chosen people call forth their gratitude and praise. They are "his chosen ones" (v. 6). The divine choice requires their obedience (v. 45) as well as their praise.

The patriarchs, God's anointed leaders (105:7–25). The psalmist recounted God's deeds in the earliest times of Israel's history. God made an everlasting covenant with Abraham, Isaac, and Jacob (vv. 8–11). He promised them the land of Canaan for an inheritance (v. 11). This promise was given while they were landless nomads (vv. 12–13). God protected them and made them the channels of His redemptive message and purpose ("prophets," v. 15).

God sent Joseph into Egypt ahead of his family and before the great famine. This proved providential. Joseph was tested and later exalted by Pharaoh. Still later, Israel came into Egypt (also called Ham in vv. 23, 27). God was preparing His people for the Exodus.

Moses and Aaron, leaders in crisis (105:26–42). These God-chosen leaders were used mightily to deliver the Hebrews from bondage. The psalmist cites eight of the plagues on Egypt, including the death of the firstborn (v. 36). The Hebrews brought booty out of Egypt in compensation for their enslavement (v. 37). After all that happened, the Egyptians were glad to see them go (v. 38). God provided for His people in the desert: the pillars of cloud and fire, quail and "bread from heaven" (*manna*), as well as water from the rock (vv. 39–41). He kept His promise to His servant Abraham (v. 42).

The reason for God's deliverance (105:43–45). God chose Israel to be His own people. He led them out of bondage with joy and singing. His providence brought them to the Land of Promise. God's grace called for the people's responsibility as well as their praise. He did all this so they would "keep His precepts, and observe His laws" (v. 45). Divine election involves both privilege and responsibility (see Amos 3:2 and Luke 12:48). God's call requires our response and faithfulness as well as our gratitude.

■ *The psalmist opened this psalm by recalling*
■ *God's mighty acts and miracles on behalf of*
■ *His people. He recounted several of God's*
■ *specific deeds in the earliest times of Israel's*
■ *history, including His covenant with Abra-*
■ *ham, promise of an inheritance, the life of*
■ *Joseph, and the Exodus. He compensated*
■ *them for their enslavement and provided for*
■ *them in the desert. God remained true to His*
■ *promise to Abraham. He chose Israel to be*
■ *His own people. This election involved both*
■ *privilege and responsibility.*

GUIDING QUESTION

Why did God deliver His people from bondage?

Background: This psalm may have been written during or after the Babylonian Exile. Parts of the psalm may have been written during David's time. Verses 47–48 appear in 1 Chronicles 16:34–36.

PSALM 106: A HISTORY OF SINFULNESS

Theme: National infidelity

Reader Insights: A hallelujah hymn. The previous psalm, Psalm 105, emphasizes God's faithfulness on behalf of His chosen people, whereas this psalm recounts His people's unfaithfulness to God.

PSALM SUMMARY

"Praise the LORD" (106:1–5). The introduction to the psalm is a call to praise prompted by God's faithfulness and mighty acts on behalf of His people. The psalmist pronounced a blessing on those who act justly and obey the divine will (v. 3). In verses 4–5 he prayed that God might remember him and deliver him when the nation is delivered.

The sins of Israel (106:6–46). Israel's sins are related by the psalmist for forty verses: "We have sinned, even as our fathers did" (v. 6). That is as true today as when the psalmist wrote it. He acknowledges both the failures of his forefathers and his own generation's responsibility. That is a mature understanding.

- *The psalmist began with a call to praise*
- *prompted by God's faithfulness and mighty*
- *acts on behalf of His people. He acknowl-*
- *edged the sins of his people and cataloged*
- *many of the sins that required God's deliver-*
- *ance and brought God's punishment.*

A concluding prayer (106:47–48). Verse 47 is a sentence prayer for salvation with the promise of praise.

Verse 48 is a doxology for Book IV of the Psalter. It blesses the Lord and calls for the people's response of praise and "Amen."

GUIDING QUESTION
What is this psalm intended to do for believers who read and ponder it?

Lessons in living: Sin contaminates. It infects not only the sinner, but may also infect the lives of others as well. Its effects can be far-reaching and long-lasting. Avoid the compromises of the world and resolve not to entertain temptation.

PSALM 107: MANKIND'S NAME IS TROUBLE

Theme: God's dependable love

Reader Insights: A hymn

PSALM SUMMARY
A call to thanksgiving (107:1–3). Let those who have experienced God's deliverance speak up. He formed the nation, bringing them to worship in the Temple.

Note how the refrain is repeated: "Let them give thanks to the LORD for his unfailing love and his wonderful deeds for men" (vv. 8, 15, 21, 31). It was sung antiphonally.

Background: This psalm is closely linked to the previous psalm and may be regarded as a continuation of the series. The psalm points to the time of the return from the Babylonian captivity.

Man, the pilgrim—God, our guide (107:4–9). The psalmist cited troubles from which God delivers His people. Men were rootless nomads, aimless wanderers, with no city to call home. They were suffering refugees who "cried out to the LORD in their trouble" (v. 6). He led them to a city.

Man, the prisoner—God, our deliverer (107:10–16). The prison (v. 10) may be literal, or it may be "the prison house of sin." In both cases, man is enslaved (v. 12). Mankind "cried to the LORD" (v. 13), and He brought them out, freed them, and pardoned them.

Man, the sufferer—God, our physician (107:17–22). Some were sin-sick and "near the gates of death" (vv. 17–18). They cried to the Lord, and He healed them (vv. 19–20).

Man, the sailor—God, our pilot (107:23–32). Verses 23–27 are vivid. Sailors in distress found that their "courage melted," and they were "at wits' end." They cried to the Lord, and He stilled the storm (as Jesus did on the Sea of Galilee).

Epilogue (107:33–43). God is Lord of both nature and the nations. He controls mankind's habitation. He provides for the needy and punishes their oppressors (vv. 39–43).

- *The psalmist began with a call for thanksgiv-*
- *ing to the God of deliverance. The psalm's*
- *theme is God's dependable love. It is*
- *unchanging, unlimited, undeserved, and*
- *always available.*

GUIDING QUESTION

What four pictures did the psalmist use to depict the frailty of man?

PSALM 108: A COMPOSITE PSALM

Background: This psalm is a combination of materials from Psalms 57 and 60. The first five verses are quoted from Psalm 57:7–11 and verses 6–13 come from Psalm 60:5–12.

Theme: A plea for help and a prayer of praise

Reader Insights: A hymn and community lament. Because this psalm is a compilation of previous psalm texts, the reader may want to see the commentary on these earlier psalms from which this one was compiled.

PSALM SUMMARY

The psalmist's faith in the midst of fear (108:1–5). The psalmist gives us the pattern of lament, confession of faith, and praise. It is repeated twice in the psalm. The psalmist sang of his steadfast faith in verse 1. He was unshaken despite the danger he faced. He could sing even in the midst of trouble.

The psalmist called for nature to awake and rejoice with him. He even went out to awaken the dawn (it usually awakens us). His joy was so complete that he could not wait for daylight to share it—like a proud father whose child has been born during the night. His thanksgiving was too good to keep to himself (v. 3). The faithfulness and love of God called forth his praise. He exalted the Lord and ascribed glory to Him "over all the earth!" (v. 5).

The oracle of God (108:6–9). God promised to restore the nation and subdue their rebellious neighboring lands. The psalm pictures God as a giant warrior who will extend His control over countries on both sides of the Jordan River. He will make Ephraim, the most powerful tribe, His helmet and Judah, King David's tribe, will become His scepter (v. 8).

Like a warrior returning from battle, God will wash His hands in the Dead Sea (in the land of Moab) and toss His shoes onto Edom. He will shout victory over the plains of Philistia (in the west). This was an early representation of the kingdom of God or His rule, which was later expanded in the New Testament.

A prayer for God's help (108:10–13). The leader prayed for the safety of a fortress city such as Petra in Edom (v. 9). He asked divine help "for the help of man is worthless" (v. 12). With God's help they could defeat their enemies (v. 13).

Thus, the psalm concluded on the glad note of expected victory. This psalm reinforces the truth of God's sovereign power. He is in control of human destiny—then and now.

■ *The psalmist was unshaken despite the dan-*
■ *ger he faced. In fact, he could sing even in the*
■ *midst of trouble. In gratitude, he lifted his*
■ *heart in praise. God promised to restore the*
■ *nation and subdue their rebellious neighbor-*
■ *ing lands. The psalmist prayed for God's*
■ *help. With His help, His people could defeat*
■ *their enemies.*

GUIDING QUESTION

What pictures did the psalmist use to describe the enemies of God's people?

PSALM 109: AN ANGRY PRAYER

Background: The psalmist was being accused with lies by his enemies. This is the prayer of a person threatened by the curse of his enemies, and it was likely spoken in the sanctuary.

Theme: Deliverance from extreme affliction

Reader Insights: An individual lament. Many commentators consider this the most severe of the "cursing psalms." The psalmist's theology obviously predates Jesus' teaching to love one's enemies (Matt. 5:44). The psalmist is fully human, and we can identify with him, perhaps a bit too readily.

PSALM SUMMARY

The psalmist's enemies (109:1–5). Enemies have proved to be "wicked and deceitful" (v. 2). They have attacked the psalmist "without cause" and returned false accusations for his love (vv. 3–4). They have rewarded him with "evil for good" and "hatred for . . . friendship" (v. 5).

A curse on his enemy (109:6–19). The psalmist pronounced a massive curse upon his enemy. This was founded not on personal vendetta, but rather on a sense of justice. (See the article "Vengeance and Vindication in the Psalms" at the back of this book.) The psalmist prayed that his enemy might be clothed in curses and soaked to the bone by them (vv. 18–19). This is a harsh prayer, indeed.

An appeal for help (109:20–31). The psalmist turned from cursing his enemy to asking God's help for himself. His own plight was pitiful: he was poor and needy (v. 22). Poverty is dehumanizing. Poverty does not equal piety. The psalmist's life was almost gone "like an evening shadow" (v. 23). His body was weak and gaunt, and he was the object of scorn (vv. 24–25). Therefore, he cried out for help (v. 26).

In conclusion the psalmist promised to praise God among the worshipers in the Temple (v. 30). God is a present help to those who are in need (v. 31).

- *Having been falsely accused, the psalmist*
- *pronounced a massive curse upon his*
- *enemy. It was bitter and harsh. Many com-*
- *mentators consider this the most severe of*
- *the "cursing psalms." The psalmist turned*
- *from cursing his enemy to asking God's help*
- *for himself. The psalmist concluded by*
- *promising to praise God among the wor-*
- *shipers in the Temple.*

GUIDING QUESTION
What is the value of bringing this kind of anger to God?

PSALM 110: KING AND PRIEST

Theme: The ultimate Priest-King, the Messiah

Reader Insights: A royal psalm. This prayer for the Davidic king typologically portrays the glory of the ultimate Davidic King, the Messiah. He is a Lord above even His father David (v. 1; Matt. 22:41–46) and a priest, though not of the Levitical line (v. 4; Heb. 7:11–28). He is the victor over all His enemies (vv. 2–3, 5–6). (See the Article "Christ in the Psalms" at the back of this book.)

PSALM SUMMARY

The king as warrior (110:1–3). The Lord spoke to His king in Zion, conferring on him authority. With the Lord's power, the King would be successful in bringing his enemies into subjection. God would enable the King to extend his rule even among his enemies. His armies will stand in readiness and he will continuously have the strength of youth.

The king as priest (110:4–7). The King was not only a warrior. He was a priest—not of the order of Aaron but of the order of Melchizedek. Melchizedek was the priest and king of Salem (Jerusalem) in Abraham's day (see Gen. 14:18–20). The Davidic kings and the Messiah were in that long line of priest-kings. They represented God to His people. God will judge the nations "on the day of his wrath" (v. 5).

Background: This was an early royal psalm used in worship at the coronation of Davidic kings perhaps as early as Solomon. Oracles from the Lord are addressed to the king by a priest or prophet. Compare this psalm with Psalm 2.

The early church saw the references in this psalm as being clearly messianic. It is the psalm most often quoted in the New Testament. Jesus quoted it (Matt. 22:44). The author of Hebrews made use of it (Heb. 1:13; 5:6; 7:17; 8:1; 10:12–13). See further references in Acts 2:34; 1 Pet. 3:22; 1 Cor. 15:25; Col. 3:1. Jesus is both our Priest and King—David's true descendant.

■ *The Davidic kings and the Messiah were in*
■ *that long line of priest-kings. The source of*
■ *their authority was God, and they repre-*
■ *sented God to His people.*

GUIDING QUESTION

What did this psalm mean to the early church?

PSALM 111: "WITH ALL MY HEART"

Theme: A personal hymn of praise to God for who He is and what He does

Reader Insights: A hallelujah hymn

PSALM SUMMARY

God's mighty works (111:1–9). The psalmist spelled out God's mighty works after a call to praise (v. 1). He generously provided food and steadfastly remembered the covenant with Israel (v. 5). God protected His people (v. 6) and established His moral law (vv. 7–8). His redemption of His people reveals His name (or character) to be holy and awe inspiring (v. 9).

The beginning of wisdom (111:10). This verse may sound strange to modern ears: "The fear of the LORD is the beginning of wisdom." The word *fear* here means "awe." Fearing and loving God are not mutually exclusive but complementary.

- *The psalmist praised God for His mighty*
- *works, listing several specific acts. The*
- *psalmist stated that the "fear" of the*
- *Lord—a reverent awe of Him—is the begin-*
- *ning of wisdom.*

GUIDING QUESTION

For what mighty works of God did the psalmist praise Him?

PSALM 112: "LIGHT IN THE DARKNESS"

Theme: The contrast between the righteous person and the wicked person

Reader Insights: A hallelujah hymn and a wisdom song

PSALM SUMMARY

A beatitude (112:1). The psalm begins with a blessing on the one who fears the Lord: "The fear of the LORD is the beginning of wisdom" (Ps. 111:10). Such a person holds God in reverence and delights to obey His commandments.

The righteous person's reward (112:2–9). The godly person will be blessed in his *posterity*. His children will be influential in the land (v. 2).

The godly person will also enjoy *prosperity*, "wealth and riches" (v. 3). Material prosperity was considered a sign of divine favor by the Hebrews. We still have similar feelings about prosperity and ask *why* when we experience adversity.

Background: In this wisdom psalm the writer contrasted the fate of the righteous man (see Ps. 1) with that of the wicked. It is an acrostic like Psalm 111, which suggests that the two poems had a common author. Compare the fates of the righteous and wicked in Proverbs 10:3–10.

God is gracious to the upright. For the godly, "in darkness light dawns" (v. 4). People of faith tend to look on the bright side and be optimistic. They see beyond surface appearances. As a response to God's blessings, the righteous person is *generous* to the poor (v. 9) and in making loans to those in need (v. 5).

The righteous person is *secure* and does not live in constant fear of bad news. "His heart is steadfast, trusting in the LORD" (v. 7). He lives not in fear but by faith (v. 8). Therefore, his strength and power (horn) endure (v. 9b).

To see a New Testament description of the wicked person, read Luke 12:13–21. This person had wealth but was not rich toward God.

The wicked person's punishment (112:10). The wicked person is angry and resentful at the prosperity and security of the godly. He will "gnash his teeth" in frustration and "waste away" and amount to nothing. The wicked person's ambition and desire "come to nothing." His fury is self-consuming. Note the contrast between generosity and resentment, the security of faith and the vanity of nonfaith.

- *The person who holds God in reverence and*
- *delights to obey His commandments will be*
- *blessed. Rewards include posterity, prosper-*
- *ity, God's grace, generosity, and security.*
- *The wicked person becomes angry and*
- *resentful at the prosperity and security of the*
- *godly. As a result, the wicked person's ambi-*
- *tion and desire "come to nothing."*

GUIDING QUESTION

How do righteous persons and wicked persons differ?

PSALM 113: GOD OF MAJESTY AND COMPASSION

Theme: Praise for God's majesty and His concern for the lowly

Reader Insights: A hallelujah hymn. The reader might want to compare this song with the song of Hannah in 1 Samuel 2:1–10.

PSALM SUMMARY

"Blessed be the name" (113:1–3). The worship leader called on the congregation, "servants of the LORD," to praise the Lord. Three times in as many verses he mentioned "the name of the LORD." God's name stands for His revealed character. Remember that in the Lord's Prayer we pray for His name to be held holy ("hallowed"). The praise of God is to go on for all eternity, "both now and forevermore!" (v. 2). The praise of God is to be universal among all people, "from the rising of the sun to the place where it sets" (v. 3).

The majestic God is concerned for the lowly (113:4–9). God is highly exalted "over all the nations." His glory is also "above the heavens" (v. 4). There is no one in all the universe who can compare with Him (v. 5).

This Lord God Almighty is aware of the plight of the poor (v. 7). He lifts them from the dust and poverty, giving them dignity. He "seats them

Background: Psalms 113–114 were sung before the Passover meal, and Psalms 115–118 were sung afterward. This would have been what Jesus and His disciples sang at the Last Supper (Matt. 26:30). This psalm is a hymn of praise to the Lord. Here God's exalted majesty and His concern for outcast humanity are combined in an important lesson.

with princes" (v. 8). The needy live on garbage thrown on the city dump (v. 7), but God cares for them.

See Mary's song, the Magnificat: "For he has been mindful of the humble state of his servant. From now on all generations will call me blessed" (Luke 1:48).

- *The worship leader called on the congrega-*
- *tion to praise the Lord. The praise of God is*
- *to be continuous; it is to go on for all eternity.*
- *No one in all the universe can compare with*
- *God. He is aware of the plight of the poor and*
- *underprivileged and cares for them.*

GUIDING QUESTION

How was this hymn used in the psalmist's day?

PSALM 114: "TREMBLE . . . AT THE PRESENCE OF THE LORD"

Theme: The Exodus

Reader Insights: A hallelujah hymn. The Exodus event was the hinge in Israel's history. Indeed, it made the nation of Israel a reality.

PSALM SUMMARY

God's deliverance of His people (114:1–8). The psalmist recounted several of the miracles of the Exodus, most of which involve water. God opened a way through the Red Sea as His people left Egypt. He parted the waters of the Jordan River so His people could walk on dry ground into Canaan. He provided Israel with water from a rock as they traveled from Egypt to Canaan. The psalmist called on the earth to tremble at the One who is sovereign over all nature.

Background: This psalm may have been written for the Passover celebration. As Psalm 113 is praise, so Psalm 114 celebrates the history of God's mighty acts on Israel's behalf. The Exodus from Egypt was to the Hebrews what Easter is to Christians. Both represent deliverance from slavery and from sin.

- *The Exodus event was the hinge in Israel's*
- *history. The psalmist recounted several of*
- *the miracles of the Exodus, giving praise to*
- *God for His mighty act of deliverance.*

GUIDING QUESTION

Describe some of the miracles associated with the Exodus.

PSALM 115: GLORY TO HIS NAME

Theme: A nation's trust in God

Reader Insights: A hallelujah hymn and a taunt song. This hymn mocks idols (and those who worship them) in the spirit of Isaiah 40:18–20 and 44:6–20.

PSALM SUMMARY

Glory belongs to God (115:1). The psalmist opened his hymn by ascribing glory to God. We are not the ones who deserve glory. It should be given to the name of God, for He alone is faithful and trustworthy. His love is always dependable.

The mockery of pagan neighbors (115:2–8). Israel's neighboring nations looked at her misfortune and asked where their God was. Such mockery was hard to take (see Ps. 79:10). The psalmist answered with humor and ridicule similar to that used in Isaiah 41 and 44. The God of heaven is sovereign and "does whatever pleases him" (v. 3). By contrast, the idols of their pagan neighbors are helpless. They are man-made

Background: This psalm and the next two were probably sung by Jesus and His disciples after the Last Supper (Mark 14:26). They were an appropriate prelude to Gethsemane and Calvary. This psalm also gives a vivid contrast between the living God and man-made idols (vv. 3–8).

gods. Their helplessness is evident in that their eyes cannot see; their mouths cannot speak. They cannot hear, smell, or help. Note the biting ridicule of verse 8: "Those who make them [idols] will be like them"—helpless!

A call to trust (115:9–18). The psalmist invited three groups to trust in the Lord. These include: the nation of Israel, the priests, and "you who fear him" (v. 11). The latter group is perhaps the devoutly religious. God had not forgotten His own (v. 12). He bestows His blessings on the "small and great alike" (v. 13), and is no respecter of persons.

The psalmist declared that the heavens belong to God, and the earth has been entrusted to mankind as a stewardship (v. 16). As far as he knew, only the living praise God (v. 17). The psalm is concluded with the people's vow to praise the Lord "forevermore" (v. 18). The principal point made by this psalm is the vivid contrast between God and the gods people make for themselves.

■ *Israel's neighboring nations looked at her*
■ *misfortune and began mocking God: "Where*
■ *is their God?" The psalmist answered with*
■ *humor and ridicule, for by contrast, the idols*
■ *of their pagan neighbors were helpless. The*
■ *psalmist invited three groups to "trust in the*
■ *LORD." These included the nation of Israel,*
■ *the priests, and those who fear the Lord. The*
■ *heavens, declared the psalmist, belong to*
■ *God, and the earth has been entrusted to*
■ *mankind as a stewardship. The people vowed*
■ *to praise God.*

GUIDING QUESTION

How did the psalmist answer the mockery of his pagan neighbors?

PSALM 116: "THE CUP OF SALVATION"

Theme: Personal thanksgiving to God

Reader Insights: An individual song of thanksgiving and a hallelujah hymn. Compare verse 3 of this hymn with Jonah 2:5, another individual song of thanksgiving.

PSALM SUMMARY

The psalmist's distress (116:1–11). The psalmist began by professing his love for the Lord, who answered his prayers (vv. 1–2). In agony he prayed that his life might be spared (v. 4). God answered by delivering him from death, wiping tears from his eyes and keeping his feet from stumbling.

The psalmist kept his faith in God, but was sorely disappointed at the attitudes of the people around him (vv. 10–11).

The psalmist's declaration of praise (116:12–19). The psalmist asked how he could repay the Lord for His goodness. He then declared he would lift the cup of salvation—a public acknowledgment of what God has done in his life. He will also bring a thank offering, call on the Lord's name, and keep his promises to the Lord. He concluded with an exclamation of praise to the Lord (v. 19).

Background: Here we have the personal testimony of a person who was seriously ill and almost died. The Lord heard his prayer and delivered him. He praised God and fulfilled his vows by bringing a sacrifice. This is a moving poem of thanksgiving in the setting of worship in the Temple.

Background: The brevity of this psalm—the shortest in the Bible—has led some to believe it is a fragment detached from its context. Indeed, some Hebrew manuscripts do not treat It as a psalm but attach it to either the end of Ps. 116 or at the beginning of Ps. 118. The message of this psalm, however, is distinct from both Pss. 116 and 118. Therefore, most regard it as a separate psalm.

■ *The psalmist professed his love for God, who*
■ *answered his prayers. Strong in his faith in*
■ *God, the psalmist expressed his dismay and*
■ *disappointment at the attitudes of those*
■ *around him who lacked faith. The psalmist*
■ *posed the rhetorical question: "How can I*
■ *repay the LORD for all his goodness to me?"*
■ *He offered his worship and expressed his*
■ *thanks to the Lord by keeping his promises.*

GUIDING QUESTION

How did the psalmist resolve to repay God for His goodness?

PSALM 117: PRAISE THE LORD, ALL NATIONS

Theme: Praise to God for His love and faithfulness

Reader Insights: A hallelujah hymn

PSALM SUMMARY

A call to praise (117:1–2). The psalmist summoned all nations and people to praise the Lord for God's deliverance and His divine purpose—their salvation. This burst of praise celebrated the eternal mercies of God.

GUIDING QUESTION

What is the point of this shortest of psalms?

PSALM 118: A PROCESSION OF PRAISE

Background: This hymn was probably sung by the king in a procession of worshipers going up to worship at the Temple. The setting for its use appears to have been the autumn Feast of Tabernacles which celebrated Israel's deliverance from Egypt.

Theme: A song of national thanksgiving

Reader Insights: An individual song of thanksgiving and an antiphonal hymn. This was Martin Luther's favorite psalm. It contains several memorable verses that are quoted in the New Testament.

PSALM SUMMARY

A litany of praise (118:1–4). The psalmist called on three groups of worshipers to respond with "His love endures forever": all Israel (v. 2), the priests (v. 3), the devout (v. 4).

The king declares Israel's faith (118:5–20). Speaking on behalf of the people, the Davidic king declared that God has heard his distress call and answered him (v. 5). With God at his side, there is nothing to fear (v. 6). Israel's refuge is in the Lord (v. 8). The nation's enemies surrounded them "like bees," but God enabled the king to "cut them off" (vv. 10–12). The Lord is the source of salvation (v. 14). He gives the victory (v. 16).

At verse 19, the procession reached the city gates of Jerusalem. The king commanded them to open, allowing the worshipers to enter and "give thanks to the LORD." The city gate was called "the gate of the LORD" because it admitted the faithful to His presence on earth within the Holy of Holies of the Temple.

Praise in the house of the Lord (118:21–29). God made the disciplined remnant of Israel "the capstone" [corner stone] (v. 22). In the Gospels, Jesus applied these verses to Himself (Mark 12:10–11). Within the Temple courtyard the priests blessed

This psalm was quoted by the Gospel writers. Here are three significant quotations from this psalm in the Gospels:

1. As the king rode into the city the priests sang, "Blessed is he who comes in the name of the LORD" (v. 26). This verse was chanted by the people who welcomed Jesus, the Prince of peace, to Jerusalem at the beginning of Holy Week (Mark 11:9).

2. Jesus applied the song of the rejected stone to Himself at the close of the parable of the vineyard keepers (vv. 22–23; Mark 12:10–11).

3. "The LORD is God, and he has made his light shine upon us" (v. 27). Jesus used the verse in His saying, "I am the light of the world" (John 8:12).

the worshipers (v. 26). This verse was quoted by the crowd when Jesus entered Jerusalem triumphantly on Palm Sunday (Matt. 21:9).

God is the source of light or spiritual truth and understanding (v. 27). The concluding verses are a jubilant statement of thanksgiving and praise to the Lord.

■ *The psalmist called on three groups of wor-*
■ *shipers to respond in praise to God. Speaking*
■ *on behalf of the people, the Davidic king*
■ *declared that God has heard his distress call*
■ *and answered him. With God at their side,*
■ *there is nothing for the nation to fear. God*
■ *made the disciplined remnant of Israel "the*
■ *capstone," or corner stone. The psalmist con-*
■ *cluded with praise to God.*

GUIDING QUESTION

What connections did the Gospel writers make to this psalm?

PSALM 119: A CELEBRATION OF THE LAW

Theme: Obedience to the law of God is the way to happiness.

Reader Insights: A Torah psalm

PSALM SUMMARY

The psalmist delights in God's Word (119:1–168). The psalmist sang the praise of the Law under all kinds of circumstances: persecution, false accusation, temptation, and intellectual doubt. Psalm 19:7–10 is restated in Psalm 119.

The Law was not a substitute for God but a guide to doing His will. It was not a burden to the psalmist but a joy. The Law enabled the psalmist to live in communion with God. It represents the written law of God, and is a dynamic communication of God's will for mankind. Sometimes the Law is also presented as "promise."

The point of the psalm is that *obedience to God's law is the way to happiness*. The poet asked divine help in understanding and keeping the law (vv. 1–8). God's Word in one's heart brings joy and protects the believer from sin (vv. 9–16). The psalmist prayed for deliverance from his enemies (vv. 25–32).

He declared his loyalty to God's law (vv. 33–40). He prayed that he might understand the law more fully (vv. 41–48). He asked that he might be able to answer his foes who taunted him (vv. 49–56).

The psalmist kept his confidence even in times of persecution (vv. 57–64). He declared his devotion to the Lord (vv. 65–72) and recognized that he could learn from what he suffered (vv. 73–80). God's ways are just (vv. 81–88). The psalmist prayed again to be delivered from his enemies (vv. 89–96).

He had an unshakable faith in the Word of God (vv. 97–104), and found the Law to be sweet and beautiful (vv. 105–112). He prayed for divine help (vv. 113–120), praying for God's intervention on his behalf (vv. 121–128). He affirmed his loyalty to the Law (vv. 129–136),

Background: This psalm, likely from postexilic times, rhymes in the original Hebrew, and it is an acrostic. This means that the psalm has twenty-two sections that correspond to the letters of the Hebrew alphabet. Each verse in this longest psalm is built around a different word that is a synonym for the word of God. These synonyms are key words throughout the psalm and include: law, word, statutes, precepts, decrees, and commands.

and praised the justice and righteousness of God's law (vv. 137–152).

The psalmist cried out to be saved from persecution (vv. 153–160) and asked that his life might be spared (vv. 161–168). He declared his own faith and devotion (vv. 169–176). He promised to sing God's praise in gratitude for divine deliverance.

Psalm 119 is the Old Testament's greatest expression of love for God's law. The psalmist meditated upon the Law, loved it, and delighted in it. Still, it is something to be obeyed. The Law is not static but *dynamic*. It provides light and guidance. Obeying the Law brings joy.

- *The psalmist sang the praise of the Law*
- *under all kinds of circumstances: persecu-*
- *tion, false accusation, temptation, and intel-*
- *lectual doubt. The psalmist delighted in the*
- *Law, as he found it provided the light and*
- *guidance he needed for his life. Most impor-*
- *tantly, obeying the Law establishes fellow-*
- *ship with the living God.*

CONCLUSION (119:168–176)

The psalmist concluded with a petition for understanding. He recommitted himself to obey the Law and confessed his reliance on the Shepherd's care (vv. 169–176). This is formal Hebrew wisdom poetry. While the psalm is repetitious, it is always true to its theme: the celebration of God's law.

GUIDING QUESTION

God's Word was of supreme importance to the psalmist. What are some of the synonyms used to describe it?

PSALM 120: THE DECEITFUL TONGUE

Background: This is one of the pilgrim psalms (Pss. 120–134). It is a kind of folk song by a person who lived far from Jerusalem and his native land. Note the title on these psalms is "a Song of Ascents." They were sung by pilgrims as they went up to Jerusalem to observe the great worship festivals.

Theme: Distress and deliverance from slanderous people

Reader Insights: An individual lament

PSALM SUMMARY

"Deliver me" (120:1–2). The psalmist was in great distress and cried out to God. His prayer was set in quotation marks in verse 2. He wanted to be delivered from persons of "lying lips" and "deceitful tongues."

A curse on his enemies (120:3–4). The psalmist prayed that his enemies might receive retribution appropriate for their offense. His enemies were shooting arrows of falsehood, trying to destroy his reputation. He asked that they be destroyed by "a warrior's sharp arrows." By their deceit they had kindled the fire of enmity against the psalmist. He prayed that they would be consumed by the hot coals of the broom tree. Like heart pine, the wood of the broom tree produced an especially hot and long-burning fire.

"Woe is me" (120:5–7). The psalmist described a foreign land of warlike people (v. 6). The nomads of Kedar lived in the desert south of Damascus (Isa. 21:13, 16–17). Meshech was an area in northern Asia Minor where the people traded in bronze vessels and slaves (Ezek. 32:26–27). The psalmist's references to the tongue are similar to what we read in the epistle of James.

- The psalmist cursed his enemies and asked
- that they receive retribution for their false-
- hoods. The psalmist lived in a foreign land
- among warlike people, and he compared his
- enemies to those people.

GUIDING QUESTION

This is the first of the Pilgrim Psalms or Songs of Ascent. What is the significance of these psalms?

PSALM 121: WHERE DO WE GO FOR HELP?

Theme: Believers have God's love and protection

Reader Insights: A processional hymn. A favorite psalm of many, it shows us God on guard. It beautifully pictures divine care and protection and answers the question: Where can we go for help?

Background: Psalm 121 was probably sung around the campfires of pilgrims en route to Jerusalem and its Temple.

PSALM SUMMARY

"I will lift up my eyes" (121:1–2). In times of crisis, we often feel threatened. It is only when we remember to look up to the hills and the One who made them that we feel secure.

God on guard (121:3–8). Six times in these verses the psalmist tells us that God keeps or protects the pilgrim. He does not let the believer's foot slip on dangerous mountain paths (v. 3). Sentries may fall asleep at their posts, but not the Lord. He watches over Israel continuously, never dozing (vv. 3–4).

He protects His own from sunstroke. He also keeps us safe from moonstroke, thought by the ancients to he harmful. Our present-day word *lunatic,* used to describe the insane, came from this belief. In day and night God keeps us safe (v. 6).

Verse 7 brings to mind the petition in the Lord's Prayer, "Deliver us from evil." He preserves our life. God watches over the pilgrims going up to Jerusalem and returning home. He protects us in our daily work, and we can trust Him for the future—"forevermore" (v. 8).

As incredible as it seems, the God who made heaven and earth cares about us individually. His love and protection are ours. That is the grand theme of this eloquent poem.

There are many hills and mountains in the Bible. But none towers higher than Calvary, where heaven and earth meet and we find our help.

■ *Where can the believer go for help? The*
■ *psalmist declared that God, "the Maker of*
■ *heaven and earth," is our personal help. God*
■ *is the guard of the righteous. Along our pil-*
■ *grim journey, we may trust Him to give us*
■ *sure footing, to be our shade, and to keep us*
■ *from evil.*

GUIDING QUESTION
What are some of the enemies from which God protects His people?

PSALM 122: PRAY FOR PEACE

Background: This psalm is a pilgrim's prayer for the peace of Jerusalem, the holy city.

Theme: The peace of Jerusalem

Reader Insights: A processional hymn. One of the Songs of Ascent.

PSALM SUMMARY

The pilgrim reaches Jerusalem (122:1–5). The psalmist was glad when his friends first suggested that he go with them to Jerusalem's Temple, "the house of the LORD" (v. 1). Perhaps he was a youth at the time. Anticipation became realization once his feet stood "in your gates, O Jerusalem" (v. 2).

The next verses are a poetic reflection on the importance of Jerusalem in the life and faith of God's people. "The tribes go up" from near and far to celebrate the presence of God in the Temple. They come to worship and "praise the name of the LORD" (v. 4). The city was also the seat of the Davidic throne (v. 5). It symbolized both religious and political unity.

Jesus may have had this psalm in mind when He wept over Jerusalem and said, "If you . . . had only known on this day what would bring you peace" (Luke 19:42).

Prayer for Jerusalem's peace (122:6–9). The psalmist encouraged his readers to "pray for the peace of Jerusalem" (v. 6). Peace (*shalom* in Hebrew) means more than the absence of strife. It also stands for health, wholeness, and well-being. "Salem" in the word *Jerusalem* means "peace." The psalmist prayed that the city might prosper and enjoy security from its enemies (v. 7). "Peace be within you" (v. 8). He wished Jerusalem well because within its city walls stood "the house of the LORD our God" (v. 9).

- *The psalmist rejoiced when his companions*
- *suggested that he journey with them to Jeru-*
- *salem. He reflected on the importance of*
- *Jerusalem in the life and faith of God's peo-*
- *ple. He encouraged his readers to pray for*
- *the peace of Jerusalem.*

GUIDING QUESTION

What made the psalmist glad?

PSALM 123: LOOK TO THE LORD

Theme: Faith in God's grace

Reader Insights: A community lament

PSALM SUMMARY

God is our help (123:1). The psalmist lifted his eyes to God "whose throne is in heaven" (v.1). This is similar to the opening phrase of the Lord's Prayer. To say that God is *transcendent* means that He surpasses our range of experience and understanding. We know of Him what He chooses to reveal.

God is merciful (123:2). The psalmist used a touching metaphor to describe the generous hand of God. We look to God for mercy as slaves look to their master.

God is gracious (123:3). The psalmist pleaded for divine grace: "Have mercy on us, O LORD" (v. 3). God was in contrast to the psalmist's enemies, who were contemptuous and scornful.

Background: The first verse is in the first person singular. It was sung by a priest. The rest of the psalm is in the first person plural and would have been sung by the worshipers.

■ *The psalmist saw God as his help in time of*
■ *need, and confidently looked to the Lord for*
■ *his deliverance. In this psalm, God's*
■ *attributes of mercy and grace are revealed.*

GUIDING QUESTION

What attributes of God are revealed in this psalm?

PSALM 124: THE LORD ON OUR SIDE

Theme: A song of thanksgiving for national deliverance

Reader Insights: A victory song

PSALM SUMMARY

God gives the victory (124:1–5). In this song of thanksgiving for national deliverance, the psalmist gave God credit for the victory. Had it not been for His divine intervention, the people of Israel would have been eaten alive by the fiery anger of their enemies (v. 3).

Israel blesses God (124:6–8). Israel blessed the Lord for not allowing them to fall prey to their enemies (v. 6). The psalmist described their deliverance as a bird escaping from the fowler's snare (v. 7). The final word is an assertion that God is Israel's help.

Background: Worshipers in the Temple prayed this song on behalf of the nation.

Fowler's Snare

A fowler is a person who traps birds. A variety of means are mentioned in Scripture: snares, ropes, and nets. God is praised as One who delivers (Pss. 91:3; 124:7) from the fowler's snare, an image of the power of the wicked.

- *In this song of thanksgiving for national*
- *deliverance, the psalmist gave God credit for*
- *saving the nation from defeat at the hands of*
- *the enemy. Israel blessed the Lord for not*
- *allowing them to fall prey to their enemies.*
- *The psalmist described their deliverance fig-*
- *uratively as a bird escaping from the*
- *fowler's snare.*

GUIDING QUESTIONS

1. What was the psalm's theme?
2. How did the psalmist describe the trouble the nation was in? What might we speculate were the kinds of dangers they were facing?
3. In what ways is this psalm applicable to believers today? What lessons might we learn from this victory song?

Psalm 125: God's Protection Surrounds Us

Background: Most affirmations of faith in the Psalms are personal. This one is on behalf of the nation. The psalm is a prayer in praise of God's protection. It expresses confidence and asks for God's help.

"City life in the ancient world was dangerous. The outside world was filled with roaming marauders, ready to attack at any sign of weakness. Constant vigilance was a prerequisite for community life. . . . Cities needed elaborate and extensive defense systems to make them safe" (Eugene H. Peterson, *A Long Obedience in the Same Direction* [Downers Grove, Ill.: InterVarsity Press, 1980), 81.

Theme: God's protection of the righteous

Reader Insights: A Zion song

PSALM SUMMARY

"Those who trust in the LORD" (125:1–3). Those who "trust in the LORD" (v. 1) are secure. They are like Jerusalem, which was situated among the hills. It was one of the safest cities because these hills provided a kind of natural fortress. The Lord is to His people what the mountains are to Jerusalem.

God's presence is His people's protection. The psalmist expressed his faith that foreign rule of the Holy Land would not last for long. Otherwise, the righteous might be tempted to despair.

"Do Good, O Lord" (125:4–5). The psalmist asked that God "do good" to His people. He prayed that God would bless "those who are upright in heart" (v. 4). They were the faithful remnant of Israel. He asked that those who were crooked or perverse be banished with the evildoers. The final line in the psalm is a prayer that peace will rest on Israel.

■ *Those who trust God are secure. They are as*
■ *firm as the mountains that surrounded Jeru-*
■ *salem. God's presence surrounds His people*
■ *and protects them. The psalmist prayed that*
■ *God would bless the upright. He concluded*
■ *with a prayer for peace upon Israel.*

GUIDING QUESTION

Why did the psalmist liken God's people to Jerusalem?

PSALM 126: THE LORD HAS DONE GREAT THINGS

Theme: Gratitude for God's gracious help

Reader Insights: A Zion song. This psalm parallels, in some sense, the reconstruction period in the southern states following the American Civil War. The Hebrew psalmist prayed for the renewal of God's favor and for prosperity to be restored.

PSALM SUMMARY

Gratitude for what the Lord has done (126:1–3). God had restored the fortunes of Zion by bringing them back from captivity in Babylon. It was like a dream come true (v. 1). Laughter and shouts of joy expressed their happiness at answered prayer. Even other nations took note of the great things the Lord had done for His people (v. 2). Israel was truly glad at His grace (v. 3).

Background: Psalm 85 is similar to this psalm, recalling past divine intervention and praying for renewal. The first three verses remember the joy of those who returned from exile in Babylon. However, their return was followed by a time of hardship and bitter disappointment.

Negev

This name means "dry." "In the rainy seasons the channels that run down from the mountains are full of water, which refreshes the soil and causes it to burst forth with fresh vegetation and flowers" (Charles A. Briggs, *The Book of Psalms,* vol. II, repr., The International Critical Commentary [Edinburgh: T & T Clark, 1986], 456).

A prayer for future renewal (126:4–6). The psalmist prayed that God might restore their fortunes again, like streams in the desert (v. 4). Verses 5–6 are a promise that those who weep as they sow will harvest with great joy.

■ *Following their return from captivity, the*
■ *psalmist prayed that God might restore the*
■ *nation's fortunes.*

GUIDING QUESTIONS

The psalmist used the image of the Negev as a symbol of renewal. What about the Negev makes this analogy effective?

PSALM 127: DEPEND ON THE LORD

Background: This short psalm is an example of the wisdom literature attributed to the wise King Solomon (note the title).

Theme: All human effort that lacks God's blessing comes to nothing.

Reader Insights: A Torah song. This psalm acclaims the value of family life under God.

PSALM SUMMARY

On building a house (127:1–2). The "house" in verse 1 may refer to the building of a dwelling or to the Temple, the house of God. He is the ultimate builder as He is the city's ultimate Watchman. Hard work and anxious toil alone will not get the job done. What is required is a combination of human effort and divine blessing: We must work as though all depends on us, and pray as if all depends on God. This is an unbeatable combination.

Working to the point of fatigue for the sake of one's family is useless. It is better to trust God and to rest in His care and protection. The psalmist reminds us that we are dependent on God (see Matt. 6:25–34). The psalmist gave a reassuring word to the insomniac: "He grants sleep to those he loves" (v. 2).

On building a home (127:3–5). Sons were regarded as a special blessing in ancient times. A man who had sons while he was still young was especially fortunate, for they gave him an advantage like sharp "arrows in the hands of a warrior." His sons would be his protection in court (at the city gate).

God is the ultimate builder of both houses and homes. He builds, watches, and gives His protection. This psalm calls on us to acknowledge our dependence on Him.

■ *Although human effort has value, we are all*
■ *dependent on God, who creates and pre-*
■ *serves life. God is the ultimate builder of both*
■ *houses and homes. We need to acknowledge*
■ *His involvement and depend on Him.*

GUIDING QUESTION

What steps might we take to ensure that we live our lives in dependence on God?

Background: The God-fearing person is the subject of this psalm (v. 1). Psalms 127 and 128 focus on the Hebrew family. Both are considered wisdom literature, the product of an Israelite sage.

Psalm 128: The Blessings of Reverence

Theme: Blessings of the God-fearing person

Reader Insights: A blessing psalm

PSALM SUMMARY

The reverent man (128:1–2). This psalm is a promise to the man who fears God and walks obediently with God. He will eat the fruit of his labor. He will be blessed materially and will also be happy and at peace (v. 2).

The godly man's family (128:3–4). The godly man's wife will be as fruitful as a vine. This was a sign of divine favor to the Hebrews. His children will be "like olive shoots" around his table. The olive tree was an evergreen, a symbol of vitality. The young shoots grew from the trunk of the tree.

A benediction (128:5–6). The last two verses are a blessing perhaps pronounced by a priest. The prayer is that God will bless this father, that he will see the prosperity of Jerusalem and that he will live to see his grandchildren.

- *The person who "fears" God is one who*
- *reveres Him and lives a life of respect and*
- *right conduct.*
- *The wife of a God-fearing man bears many*
- *children. This was seen by the Hebrews as a*
- *sign of God's favor.*

GUIDING QUESTION

What does God promise to the person who fears Him?

PSALM 129: THE ENEMIES OF ISRAEL

Theme: Israel's suffering at the hands of her enemies

Reader Insights: A psalm of national curses

PSALM SUMMARY

Persecuted but preserved (129:1–4). Despite all that Israel had suffered at the hands of her enemies, God had kept her. The young nation came out of Egypt (see Hos. 11:1). Many tried to destroy the Israelites: the Egyptians, Canaanites, Philistines, Assyrians, and Babylonians.

The psalmist described the suffering of Israel at the hands of her enemies as being plowed with long furrows. But God kept His people in spite of their persecution at the hands of many foes (v. 4).

A curse on their enemies (129:5–8). The psalmist prayed that God would bring shame on Israel's enemies (v. 5). He asked that they wither like shallow-rooted grass that grows on the flat roof (v. 6), never producing hay or grain (v. 7). Israel's enemies will never enjoy "the blessing of the LORD" (v. 8). The people of God persevere and will not know ultimate destruction (see Matt. 16:18).

Background: Israel's enemies had been a problem to the nation, as this lament indicates. Still, the Lord had preserved her. This psalm is similar to Ps. 124 in thought and style.

■ *The psalmist described the suffering of Israel*
■ *at the hands of her enemies. But God has kept*
■ *her despite her many persecutions. The*
■ *psalmist pronounced a curse on Israel's ene-*
■ *mies. He asked that they wither like shallow*
■ *rooted grass that grows on the flat roof,*
■ *never producing hay or grain (v. 7).*

GUIDING QUESTION

How did the psalmist describe the treatment of Israel at the hands of her enemies?

PSALM 130: "OUT OF THE DEPTHS"

Background: In historic Christian usage, this is one of the seven penitential psalms (or psalms of repentance; see also Pss. 6; 32; 38:51; 102; 143). It comes from the psalmist's dark distress and sounds the notes of hope and forgiveness.

Theme: A plea for forgiveness

Reader Insights: An individual lament

PSALM SUMMARY

"Out of the depths" (130:1–2). The psalmist's distress stemmed from his sin and alienation from God. His problem was guilt, and his need was forgiveness from God. He cried from the depths of despair like a drowning man. He pleaded that God would hear and answer his supplications.

God of grace (130:3–4). Having confessed his need and having entered a plea for pardon, the psalmist next magnified God's graciousness. If God gave us what we deserved, "who could stand?" (see Gal. 2:16; Rom. 3:20). But God forgives (see Ps. 86:5), and this inspires our reverence and gratitude (v. 4). "Fear" in this verse means obedience and devotion, which is inspired by divine forgiveness. Jesus taught that those who have been forgiven much, love much.

Waiting for the Lord (130:5–6). In great expectation the psalmist waited for the word of divine pardon. That was his hope and his salvation. He was as anxious to hear the word of the Lord as the weary night watchman is to see the dawn.

The nation's hope (130:7–8). Salvation is corporate as well as individual. God was concerned with the salvation of the nation of Israel as well as individuals within it. Only God can redeem His people from their sins (Mark 10:45). Israel's hope was in the Lord (v. 7). His love is dependable and His forgiveness is adequate.

- *In great distress, the psalmist cried from the*
- *depths of despair, seeking God's forgiveness.*
- *Drawing from his understanding of God's*
- *character, the psalmist next magnified God's*
- *graciousness. The fact of God's forgiveness*
- *inspired his obedience and devotion. The*
- *psalmist's hope and salvation were tied to his*
- *expectation of divine pardon for his sin. God*
- *was concerned with the salvation of the nation*
- *of Israel as well as individuals within it.*

GUIDING QUESTION
In what circumstances did the psalmist find himself?

Background: This psalm is attributed to David. Scholars find confirmation of this in the remark of David recorded in 2 Sam. 6:21.

PSALM 131: SUBMISSION TO GOD'S WILL

Theme: A humble spirit of submission to God's will

Reader Insights: A testimony song

PSALM SUMMARY

Contentment (131:1–3). The psalmist had learned to live within his capabilities and to be content with his lot in life. Once he had been proud and haughty. Now he had a more realistic self-understanding. This brought peace. Many people are "walking civil wars" because they have such low self-esteem or unrealistic ambitions. The psalmist's soul was as calm as a quieted child at its mother's breast (v. 2). The third verse is a call for Israel to "hope in the LORD."

- The psalmist had learned to live within his
- capabilities and to be content with his lot in
- life. He was at peace with himself. He closed
- his psalm by calling Israel to hope in the Lord.

GUIDING QUESTION

What was the source of peace in the psalmist's life?

PSALM 132: DAVID AND THE LORD

Background: This is a royal psalm written prior to the Exile in Babylon. It focuses on the ark of the covenant and King David's desire to build a Temple to house it (see 2 Sam. 7).

Theme: David's desire to build a Temple to house the ark of the covenant

Reader Insights: A Zion song

PSALM SUMMARY

King David's desire (132:1–5). The psalmist reminded the Lord of the hardships David endured in his desire to build a sanctuary for the ark of the covenant (see 1 Chron. 22:14). He vowed to transfer the ark to Jerusalem (vv. 3–5) and to establish "a dwelling for the Mighty One of Jacob" (see 2 Sam. 7:1–2). The psalmist asked that David's determination be remembered, not only for his sake but also for the favor of succeeding Davidic kings (see v. 10).

The Ark of the Covenant

The ark of the covenant names the original container for the Ten Commandments and the central symbol of God's presence with the people of Israel. The origin of the ark goes back to Moses at Sinai. The ark was designed for mobility. Its size (about four feet long, two and one-half feet wide, and two and one-half feet deep) and rectangular shape were appropriate to this feature. Permanent poles were used to carry the ark, since no one was allowed to touch it, and only priestly (Levitical) personnel were allowed to carry it.

Reenacting the ark's removal (132:6–10). A choir abruptly entered the psalm at this point. This leads us to believe that there must have been a dramatic processional in which the transfer of the ark to Jerusalem was reenacted by worshipers. David had heard of the ark while in his hometown of Bethlehem, called Ephrathah (v. 6). He located the ark in the fields of Jaar, a poetic abbreviation of Kiriathjearim (see 2 Sam. 6:2–12).

Notice the quotation marks in verse 7. The choir called on other worshipers to go up to Jerusalem and worship "at his footstool" (the ark that represents the Lord's dwelling place on earth).

■ *The Lord was reminded of the hardships*
■ *David had endured in his desire to build a*
■ *sanctuary for the ark of the covenant. The*
■ *psalmist asked that David's determination be*
■ *remembered, not only for his sake but also*
■ *for the favor of succeeding Davidic kings.*
■ *The text leads us to believe that worshipers*
■ *took part in a dramatic processional in*
■ *which the transfer of the ark to Jerusalem*
■ *was reenacted.*

God chose David and Zion (132:11–18). This portion of the psalm contains two oracles. The first is God's promise to David (vv. 11–12; 2 Sam. 7:2–17). God said He would put one of David's sons on the throne after him (v. 11). This promise reached its fulfillment in Christ, who was obedient unto death.

The second oracle tells how God chose Zion or Jerusalem as "his dwelling" (v. 13). The Lord promised to dwell there and to abundantly "bless" the city. Her poor would be provided bread (v. 15). Jerusalem's priests would be clothed with salvation, and its "saints" (the devout believers; see 30:4) would "sing for joy" (v. 16).

The power of David's "horn" would be great, and his "lamp" would not go out (v. 17). The king was promised that his enemies would be defeated and that his own crown would not lose its luster (v. 18). Such promises were transferred in Christian thought from David and Zion to Christ and the church. God is present today in His Son and in His body of believers.

GUIDING QUESTION
What did the ark of the covenant represent?

PSALM 133: LIVING TOGETHER IN UNITY

Theme: Unity among believers

Reader Insights: A wisdom psalm

Background: This psalm originates with wisdom teachers.

PSALM SUMMARY

The wisdom of unity (133:1–2). This wisdom psalm focuses on family unity—peace among brothers. There is often rivalry between brothers, both blood brothers and spiritual brothers.

The psalmist said that unity among brethren is like the fragrant oil used to anoint Aaronic priests at their ordination. It flowed like perfume from their head down to the candidate's full beard. Unity is like the refreshing and life-giving dew on Mount Hermon, the most prominent mountain north of the Promised Land. Often snow-capped, it is in view from much of Galilee on a clear day.

"My prayer is not for them alone. I pray also for those who will believe in me through their message, that all of them may be one, Father, just as you are in me and I am in you. May they also be in us so that the world may believe that you have sent me" (John 17:20–21).

Unity within the family of God (133:3). Unity in Zion and within the family of God is a blessing, "life forevermore" (v. 3).

- *The psalmist focused on family unity and*
- *peace among God's people. Unity in Zion and*
- *within the family of God is a blessing. In the*
- *New Testament this fellowship between fel-*
- *low believers, brethren, is called koinonia or*
- *Christian fellowship.*

GUIDING QUESTION

How did the psalmist describe unity among God's people?

PSALM 134: A PSALM OF BLESSING

Background: This is the last Psalm of Ascent to Jerusalem (Pss. 120–134). It was nighttime. The congregation was about to leave the crowded courts of the Temple at the close of a day of worship. This psalm was a parting salutation and charge to those who remained in the Temple.

Theme: Benediction asking God's blessing on worshipers in the Temple

Reader Insights: A hymn. The first two verses are a hymn calling on worshipers to "praise the LORD." Verse 3 is a prayer (probably by the priests) that God would bless the people.

PSALM SUMMARY

"Praise the LORD" (134:1–2). The psalmist invited the "servants of the LORD" to worship and "praise the LORD." Night services were held in the Temple during the autumn Feast of Tabernacles (v. 1). Lifting the hands was the attitude of prayer among the Jews (see Ps. 28:2; 1 Tim. 2:8).

"May the LORD . . . bless you" (134:3). This benediction asked that God bless the worshipers "from Zion." The Lord who made heaven and earth dwells in the Holy of Holies. God's blessings are both particular and universal.

■ *The psalmist invited the "servants of the*
■ *LORD" to worship at services held in the*
■ *Temple during the autumn Feast of Taberna-*
■ *cles. The psalm concluded with a benediction*
■ *asking God to bless worshipers from Zion.*

Lessons in living: Believers should be encouraged that God hears their prayers and praise at all times. We are assured of His blessing.

GUIDING QUESTION

What is the setting for this psalm?

PSALM 135: A HYMN OF PRAISE TO GOD

Theme: Praise for God

Reader Insights: A hymn and taunt song. A *taunt* song reproached the godless for their vile behavior and promised that their doom was near.

PSALM SUMMARY

"Praise the LORD" (135:1–4). This is a call to worship and praise. It is directed to the priests and worshipers who stand in the Temple (v. 2). God's name is to be praised because He is good (v. 3) and because by His grace He chose Israel for His own (v. 4).

Why we praise the Lord (135:5–18). The psalmist spelled out the reasons for mankind's praise of God: (1) He is Lord of creation (vv. 5–7). (2) God is Lord of history. He delivered Israel from slavery in Egypt. He subdued their enemies and gave them a good land as a heritage (vv. 8–12). (3) He is superior to all gods (vv. 15–18).

Concluding summons to praise (135:19–21). The psalmist addressed this call to worship to the house of Israel or the nation, to the priests ("house of Aaron," v. 19), and to their assistants (the Levites, v. 20). The final verse blesses the Lord "who dwells in Jerusalem" (v. 21). God is to be praised by mankind for who He is and what He does.

Background: This is a hymn of praise to God as the Lord of both creation and history. Scholars think it dates from a time after the Exile in Babylon. It is a combination of other psalms and Old Testament passages skillfully woven together.

■ *The psalmist spelled out several reasons for*
■ *mankind's praise of God: He is Lord of cre-*
■ *ation; God is Lord of Hebrew history; and He*
■ *is mightier than all pagan deities. The*
■ *psalmist issued a concluding summons to*
■ *praise God.*

GUIDING QUESTION

This is a taunt song. What is the purpose for this kind of psalm?

PSALM 136: "HIS STEADFAST LOVE"

Background: This is a worship hymn that was used at the great festivals. It was called the Great Hallel (Praise) and is similar to Ps. 135 in content—a thanksgiving to God as Lord of creation and history. The psalm has a familiar refrain, "His love endures forever," which is repeated in each verse. This probably indicates that it was sung antiphonally by the choir and congregation or by a worship leader and the choir.

Theme: God's unchanging love for His people

Reader Insights: An antiphonal hymn

PSALM SUMMARY

Call to give thanks (136:1–3). The psalmist called the congregation to praise the Lord because of His goodness and His superiority to all gods.

God and Creation (136:4–9). The psalmist focused on God as Creator of the earth, sun, moon, and stars.

God and Israel (136:10–26). The psalmist rehearsed God's mighty acts in the history of His people, Israel: God struck down the firstborn of Egypt and brought the Hebrews out of bondage. He "divided the Red Sea," enabling Israel to pass through it in safety. He then overthrew Pharaoh's army in the sea. God sustained and guided His people in the desert as they traveled from Egypt to Canaan. By His help mighty kings were defeated and Israel received the land "as an inheritance" (v. 21).

A splendid line occurs in verse 25: He "gives food to every creature." This speaks of God's universal providence. He not only made everything and everyone, but He also sustains and provides for all. The final verse (v. 26) is a summons to thanksgiving.

This is the only place in the Psalms in which the Lord is called "the God of heaven."

- The psalmist rehearsed God's mighty acts in
- creation and in the history of Israel. God's
- providence in the past gives us confidence to
- trust Him today and to hope for the future.

GUIDING QUESTION
What do God's mighty acts on behalf of Israel mean to us today?

PSALM 137: HOMESICK

Theme: Anger and grief over being exiled in Babylon

Reader Insights: A national curse

PSALM SUMMARY
"By the rivers of Babylon" (137:1–6). The psalmist found himself living along the Tigris and Euphrates rivers in Babylon. He had carried his stringed instrument with him into exile. The psalmist and his companions sat in the dust and mourned. They remembered Zion (the city of Jerusalem with its Temple) and hung their harps on the trees which grew along the river banks

Background: The historical setting of this psalm is the conquest of Jerusalem in 586 B.C. The Babylonians carried off the most skilled and intelligent Judeans into exile. These people felt literally cut off from God, whom they thought dwelled in their holy city, Jerusalem. The poem reflects religious homesickness. The psalmist must have been a victim of the Exile himself—numbered among those in the foreign land.

(v. 2). In only a few words, the psalmist pictured the sad scene.

Insult was added to grief when their captors tormented them with a demand for music and mirth (v. 3). Perhaps the Babylonians found the Jewish Temple music quaint and amusing. However, the psalmist found it difficult to sing the Lord's songs in a foreign land (v. 4).

The psalmist pronounced a curse on himself if he should ever forget Jerusalem, his spiritual home. The results of the curse sound like those of a stroke victim: may his right hand, with which he played, be paralyzed and wither away; may his tongue cleave to the roof of his mouth, leaving him unable to speak or sing. He will not be a traitor to Jerusalem.

A curse on the enemies of God (137:7–9). The psalmist prayed that the Lord would remember the treachery of their neighbors, the Edomites. They were the blood brothers of the Judeans—descendants of Esau, the brother of Jacob. The Edomites had gloated when Jerusalem fell, saying, "Tear it down to its foundations!" (v. 7; see Joel 3:19; Jer. 49:7–22). Enmity between the Jews and Arabs is centuries old.

The psalmist also cursed Babylon (v. 8). He cursed them by pronouncing a blessing on whoever conquered Babylon and repaid them for their cruelty. Those were crude and cruel times. The psalmist not only longed for Jerusalem; he also longed for the Lord to do justice by repaying Babylon in kind.

- *The psalmist found himself living along the*
- *Tigris and Euphrates rivers in Babylon,*
- *where he sat in the dust and wept. He pro-*
- *nounced a curse on himself if he should ever*
- *forget Jerusalem, his spiritual home.*
- *The psalmist prayed that the Lord would*
- *remember the treachery of their neighbors.*
- *He then cursed Babylon by pronouncing a*
- *blessing on whoever conquered Babylon and*
- *repaid them for their cruelty to the people of*
- *Judah.*

GUIDING QUESTION

Why was the psalmist so grieved?

PSALM 138: A PRAYER OF GRATITUDE

Background: This is the first of eight psalms of David (138–145).

Theme: Thanksgiving to God

Reader Insights: An individual song of thanksgiving. The psalmist was grateful that the Lord had answered his prayers and delivered him from trouble.

PSALM SUMMARY

"I will praise you, O LORD" (138:1–3). The psalmist stood in the Temple courtyard, giving thanks to God with his "all his heart" (v. 1). The "gods" in verse 1 may refer to the angels or pagan deities. The psalmist bowed toward the Holy of Holies and praised God for His steadfast love and faithfulness. God had answered his cry (v. 3).

"May all the kings of the earth praise you" (138:4–8). These verses sound much like Psalm 23, where the psalmist affirmed his faith in God, who preserved his life in troubled times. God had a purpose for his life and had delivered him from his enemies. His final prayer was that God would not forsake him since he was the "work" of the Almighty's hands. God had made him and values him.

- *The psalmist gave praises to God for His love*
- *and faithfulness. God answered his prayer.*
- *The psalmist affirmed his faith in God. His*
- *final prayer is that God will not forsake him*
- *since he is the "work" of God's hands.*

GUIDING QUESTION

On what basis did the psalmist appeal to God not to forsake him?

PSALM 139: "WHERE SHALL I GO FROM YOUR SPIRIT?"

Background: This is the second of eight psalms of David in this section of the Psalter. It is one of the most profoundly introspective sections of Scripture.

Theme: The omniscient and omnipresent God

Reader Insights: A song of trust. The author of the poem knew the Lord intimately. It is a powerful affirmation of faith. The psalm celebrates God's knowledge, power, and presence.

PSALM SUMMARY

God's unlimited knowledge (139:1–6). God knows all about us—everything we have ever thought or done, whether good or bad. He knows the intentions of our hearts, our very motives, which may not even be known to us.

God's universal presence (139:7–12). There may have been a time in the psalmist's life when he felt guilty and had tried to escape or hide from God. He learned that such is impossible; there can be no secret crimes. One cannot evade "the Hound of Heaven."

God is everywhere, the psalmist declared. He is in heaven and in Sheol, the abode of the dead (not hell). There is no running away from God any more than a person can run away from oneself. No matter where we are, His hand will lead us, and His right hand will hold us (v. 10).

Even darkness does not hide us from God. The dark is like light to Him (v. 12). God's presence can haunt us. It may be unwelcome and unwanted; however, there is also great security in His presence. He is with us, protecting us, loving us, even when we may not want Him.

God made us and we are His (139:13–18). The psalmist marveled at God's creation in the birth process. Thoughtful persons still do (see Job 10:8–11). In beautiful, poetic language God is said to have "knit" the psalmist together in his mother's womb (v. 13). Thus, the Lord knew him from the beginning (v. 14).

God saw the psalmist as an embryo long before any person saw evidence of his development inside his mother's body. Also, God recorded his development day by day—a fascinating process we now know about.

The psalmist was stunned at the magnitude of God's thoughts. The more we learn about the human body and the natural world, the more we should stand in awe and worship. Waking or sleeping, God is there (v. 18).

God, the universal Judge (139:19–24). Vengeance belongs to God. He alone can judge correctly, for He knows all the circumstances and our inner motives. The wicked are considered God's enemies. The psalmist saw them as his own, as well (vv. 21–22).

The concluding verses are a beautiful prayer (vv. 23–24). The psalmist was keenly aware of his own imperfection and of his desire to do right: "Search me, O God, and know my heart; test me and know my anxious thoughts."

He then asked that God would "see if there is any offensive way in me." The New English Bible translates it, "any path that grieves you." He concluded by praying, "Lead me in the way everlasting" or in the ancient way (see Jer. 6:16). These verses acknowledge the believer's dependence on God, which is at the heart of faith.

Psalm 139 is an incomparable lyric of God's presence. Historically, this psalm has been used in Christian worship at Easter (as Ps. 22 is associated with the cross). It reminds us that in His Incarnation Jesus knows us, for He became what we are (human). The verse "when I awake, I am still with you" (v. 18) has been applied to the resurrection. The psalm celebrates God's knowledge and His creative power, as well as His moral correction.

- *God knows all about us. He is acquainted*
- *with all our ways, our deeds and thoughts.*
- *God is everywhere. For those who do not*
- *welcome Him, there is no escaping Him. For*
- *those who desire God's presence, this fact is*
- *a promise. The psalmist marveled at God's*
- *creation in the birth process. Clearly, the*
- *psalmist was stunned at the magnitude of*
- *God's thoughts. Vengeance belongs to God.*
- *He alone can judge correctly, for He knows*
- *all the circumstances and our inner motives.*
- *The psalmist acknowledged his dependence*
- *on God.*

GUIDING QUESTION

What are some of the implications of God's being all-knowing?

PSALM 140: "RESCUE ME, O LORD"

Theme: Prayer for deliverance and vindication

Reader Insights: An individual lament. The psalmist prayed that God would deliver him from his enemies—and punish them.

PSALM SUMMARY

"Rescue me" (140:1–8). The psalmist prayed to be delivered from enemies plotting his destruction. They were evil and violent. He used two metaphors to describe their speech: *sharp* like a knife and *poisonous*.

They were like skilled hunters who set a trap and a net to ensnare him (v. 5). He prayed that God would hear his cry (v. 6) and prevent his enemies from succeeding in their destructive schemes (v. 8).

"Prayer for vindication" (140:9–11). The psalmist prayed that what his enemies had planned for him would come back on them. He wanted to see God remove liars and violent men from the land.

God is just (140:12–13). The psalmist was convinced that God would champion the cause of the poor who are hounded by their enemies. The righteous will walk in God's presence, praising Him continually.

■ *The psalmist prayed to be delivered from and*
■ *protected from evil, violent men. The psalm-*
■ *ist prayed that the curse of his enemies might*
■ *be poured out on their own heads and that*
■ *they would be destroyed. Convinced that*
■ *God would champion the cause of the righ-*
■ *teous who are afflicted by their enemies, the*
■ *psalmist gave thanks for God's deliverance.*

GUIDING QUESTION

What were the characteristics of the psalmist's enemies?

Background: The psalmist appears to have been a young man in danger of being influenced by wicked men. He was concerned about the potential for their negative influence in his life. But he had the presence of mind and maturity of faith to ask for God's help in resisting temptation.

The psalmist's prayer in this psalm is a preventive one. He recognized the attraction and peril for temptation and prayed for deliverance from it. Certainly, this is a wiser prayer than yielding to temptation and then having to turn to God in repentance (Ps. 51). Jesus taught His disciples to take action to prevent sin: "If your hand or your foot causes you to sin, cut it off and throw it away. It is better for you to enter life maimed or crippled than to have two hands or two feet and be thrown into eternal fire. And if your eye causes you to sin, gouge it out and throw it away. It is better for you to enter life with one eye than to have two eyes and be thrown into the fire of hell" (Matt. 18:7–9).

Theme: God's rule can allow no rival, whether enemies or evil.

Reader Insights: An individual lament

PSALM SUMMARY

Prayer as worship (141:1–2). The psalmist issued an urgent call for God to hear and answer his request. He prayed with uplifted hands and likened his petition to the evening sacrifice (see Exod. 29:38–42).

The gift of silence (141:3–4). The psalmist was tempted to make an impression on rich but evil men by the use of his glib tongue. Perhaps he was being drawn into their lewd talk and callous attitudes that showed no regard for God. He prayed that God would control what he said. The psalmist also prayed that he might not be tempted by the fancy foods and social life of the wicked (v. 4).

Overcoming temptation (141:5–10). The psalmist declared that it is better to be rebuked by a good person than to be praised by a person who is evil (v. 5). The anointing with perfumed oil was a courtesy shown guests at a banquet (Ps. 23:5). The psalmist prayed for the destruction of evil people (v. 7). He also asked that evildoers might not catch him in temptation's trap (v. 9), but that their evil schemes might boomerang on them (v. 10; 140:9).

- *The psalmist opened his psalm with a call to*
- *God to accept his prayer as incense and the*
- *lifting of his hands as an offering of evening*
- *sacrifice. The psalmist asked God to guard*
- *his speech and not allow his heart to be*
- *drawn to evil motives and actions. As a pre-*
- *ventive measure, the psalmist prayed for the*
- *destruction of evil people and for his own*
- *deliverance from the traps of temptation.*

GUIDING QUESTION

What petition in Jesus' Model Prayer does this psalm bring to mind?

PSALM 142: "NO MAN CARES FOR ME"

Background: This psalm is appropriate to the occasion mentioned in the superscription, "A *maskil* of David. When he was in the cave." The lonely and distressed psalmist poured out his heart before the Lord in this psalm. His great loneliness stemmed from the feeling that nobody cared whether he lived or died. He agonized in prayer.

Theme: A plea for God's help

Reader Insights: An individual lament

PSALM SUMMARY

The psalmist's lament (142:1–4). The psalmist came to the Lord overwhelmed and feeling the weakness of his humanity (v. 3). He came to God and bared his soul, complaining and begging for mercy (vv. 1–2). The psalmist's enemies were out to trap him (v. 3*b*). He looked to his right for protection, for a friend, someone to help. But he concluded that no one cared about him (v. 4). He felt utterly forsaken.

The psalmist's refuge (142:5–7). He had the good sense to turn to the Lord in his loneliness and despair (v. 5). He told God exactly what his situation was—both on the outside as well as how he felt. He asked God to bring him out of the prison he was in. The result would be thanksgiving to God and recognition of his friends that God had acted on his behalf (v. 7).

■ *The psalmist turned to the Lord in his loneli-*
■ *ness and despair. He found bright hope even*
■ *in the darkness of his lament.*

GUIDING QUESTION

What did the psalmist do that is worthy of emulation?

Psalm 143: "No One Living Is Righteous Before You"

Theme: A call for God's help

Reader Insights: An individual lament

PSALM SUMMARY

Background: There are seven psalms of penitence: 6, 32, 38, 51, 102, and 130. This is the last of the group.

A cry for help (143:1–2). The psalmist prayed that God would hear his prayer and act. He asked God not to judge him because he was keenly aware that he fell short of God's righteousness (see Rom. 3:20; Gal. 2:16).

The psalmist's need (143:3–6). His enemies had hounded him, knocked him to the ground, and caused him to live in darkness like that of death. (v. 3*b*). He was exhausted from the chase (v. 4).

The psalmist knew God could help. He remembered God's mighty acts in times past and so called out to God as the parched soil thirsts for rain (v. 6).

- Pursued by his enemies, the psalmist recalled
- God's mighty acts of the past. He was greatly
- encouraged by God's history of deliverance.

The psalmist's petition (143:7–12). The psalmist expressed his complete dependence on God. He recognized his need for awareness of God's unfailing love, for the heart to do God's will and the knowledge of what that will is, for deliverance from enemies, and a consistent walk.

The psalmist's motive was God's glory—that God's character would be recognized and honored among those who witness what God does. In a final appeal, the psalmist prayed that God would deliver him "for your name's sake . . . in your righteousness . . . in your unfailing love" (vv. 11–12). He also asked for the destruction of his enemies.

He made an honest appeal to God, asking for divine guidance and deliverance. He longed for the presence of God in his life, as well as to be rescued.

■ *The psalmist's need was urgent. He made an*
■ *honest appeal to God and prayed that He*
■ *would deliver him and destroy his enemies.*

GUIDING QUESTIONS

1. What was the psalmist's prayer?
2. The psalmist wanted God to hear his prayer. Why was he encouraged to continue to place his confidence in God?
3. In his final appeal, the psalmist prayed that God would deliver him. What attributes of God's character did he cite?

Lessons in Living: In his time of need, the psalmist remembered God's mighty acts in times past. We may be encouraged in the same way. God's providential care in days past gives us confidence that He will do the same today and in the days ahead.

PSALM 144: VICTORY AND PROSPERITY

Theme: Joy in God's protection

Reader Insights: A prayer for victory. The martial spirit of this prayer is tempered by the fact that the object of victory was not conquest or military honor but security for the people.

PSALM SUMMARY

A royal prayer (144:1–11). This is obviously the prayer of a soldier, a warrior-king. He credited God with teaching him the skills of warfare (v. 1). God was also his security: "My fortress, my stronghold and my deliverer, my shield." "Deliverer" means literally "my deliverer for myself." It was the Lord who gave the psalmist victory, enabling him to subdue other nations (v. 2).

Verses 3–4 sound much like Psalm 8, asking, "What is man . . . or the son of man?" The psalmist concluded that man, including the king, "is like a breath; his days are like a fleeting shadow" (v. 4). Life is transitory. This is one of the themes found often in the Psalter.

The king prayed that God would "part" the heavens "and come down" (v. 5). God did precisely that at the birth of Jesus. He prayed that God would come in might, causing volcanoes to erupt and sending a storm whose flashing lightning would be like arrows. At the Incarnation God came in a lowly fashion, not as people expected Him to come. God often surprises us.

The king prayed for victory over his treaty-breaking enemies (vv. 7–8). He promised to "sing a new song to . . . God," accompanied by "a ten-stringed lyre [harp]" (v. 9). It is God

Background: This hymn is largely a mosaic of citations from other psalms. We have a combination of two kinds of psalms here. The first half is a royal psalm (vv. 1–11). The second portion is wisdom poetry (vv. 12–15). This psalm may have been used as a coronation song.

who gives victories to kings and who rescues and delivers His people (vv. 10–11).

■ *The warrior-king in this section credited*
■ *God with teaching him the skills of warfare.*
■ *He knew his security was not his own might,*
■ *but God. He prayed for victory over his*
■ *treaty-breaking enemies.*

A prayer for prosperity (144:12–15). This wisdom psalm is beautiful. As noted above, it may have been used as a coronation song. The psalmist asked that their sons might be vigorous and their daughters stately (v. 12). The people also prayed for bumper crops and fertile flocks (vv. 13–14). They asked for peace and freedom from crisis: "There will be . . . no cry of distress in our streets" (v. 14b).

The concluding line is a triumphant benediction: "Blessed are the people whose God is the LORD" (v. 15b). This psalm is a prayer for victory in war and prosperity in peacetime. Both are God's undeserved grace to His people.

■ *The psalmist prayed for prosperity for his*
■ *people: that their sons might be vigorous and*
■ *their daughters stately. He concluded with a*
■ *triumphant benediction.*

GUIDING QUESTIONS

1. What is the background for this psalm?
2. The king was vivid in his descriptions of God's protection. How does God protect His people?

Lessons in Living: God takes great personal interest in His own because of His lovingkindness. Our personal joy in God is founded on what He does and who He is. God's people are recipients of God's grace.

3. What do we learn from the psalmist's wisdom psalm in vv. 12–15?

PSALM 145: "I WILL BLESS YOUR NAME FOREVER"

Background: A profound hymn, this psalm was probably used as a solo in Temple worship (v. 1). Its date of composition is thought to be after the Exile.

Theme: Praise for the glory and majesty of God

Reader Insights: A hymn. This acrostic psalm (each verse begins with the succeeding letter of the Hebrew alphabet) features the character of Israel's God and His kingdom. This psalm is readily understood and loved by Christians, as it was by ancient Jews.

PSALM SUMMARY

The promise to praise God (145:1–3). The psalmist promised to praise the Lord "every day" and "for ever." The reason for his praise was the greatness of God. "Great is the LORD and most worthy of praise" (v. 3).

The wondrous works of God (145:4–7). God is our Creator and our Redeemer. Each generation will remember and proclaim His "mighty acts." Interestingly, the works of God cause us to stand in awe (v. 6), and they call forth our praise (v. 7).

The compassion of God (145:8–9). "The Lord is gracious and compassionate." His anger does not have a short fuse, and His love knows no limits. God is not only merciful to His own people. "The LORD is good to all" (v. 9).

The kingdom of God (145:10–13). The kingdom of God means His reign, the area where He rules as Lord. It is made up of individuals who submit

God's Compassion

God's compassion is an extension of His mercy. God is tenderhearted and He demonstrates loving compassion for His people (Exod. 3:7; Ps. 103:13). This includes His slowness toward anger and wrath, which is His persistent love (Rom. 2:4; 2 Pet. 3:9). If grace is giving us what we do not deserve, God's mercy includes not giving us what we deserve.

to His lordship and is as broad as the church, made up of all born-again believers.

All the faithful bless the Lord (v. 10). They declare "the glory of your kingdom" (v. 11). God's kingdom "endures through all generations" (that is, it lasts forever, v. 13). We know this is true because He gives eternal life to all who believe in Him. (Note that v. 13 is quoted in Dan. 4:3, 34.)

God's Faithfulness

This is another of God's great attributes. God's faithfulness is closely related to His consistency. His will and actions are always found true, reliable, and steadfast. He will never commit Himself to do something He is not capable of doing (Lam. 3:23–24; 1 Thess. 5:24).

■ *The kingdom of God means His reign, the*
■ *area where He rules as Lord. It is made up of*
■ *individuals who submit to His lordship and is*
■ *as broad as the church, made up of all*
■ *born-again believers.*

The faithfulness of God (145:14–21). God is faithful in both His words and His deeds (v. 13c). He lifts up the fallen (v. 14). He provides food for all (v. 15). "Every living thing" receives from the bounty of God's hand (v. 16). The Lord is just and kind, a wonderful combination (v. 17). He "is near to all who call on him" (v. 18). To call God "Father" means that He is accessible. God hears the cry of those in distress and saves them (v. 19). He preserves those who love Him but will destroy the rebellious (v. 20).

The psalm ends as it began, with the promise of praise and an invitation for "all flesh" to "praise his holy name for ever and ever" (v. 21).

- *God is faithful in both His words and His*
- *deeds, a great truth that is documented*
- *throughout Scripture. That God's people*
- *may call God "Father" means that He is*
- *accessible—another great truth.*

GUIDING QUESTIONS

1. This psalm is an acrostic. Why were some psalms given this form?

2. The psalmist praised God for His love. What did he tell us about God's love?

3. The psalmist also praised God for His faithfulness. What did he tell us about this attribute of God?

Lessons in Living: It is difficult for finite human beings to comprehend God's attributes. We can conclude that all His attributes work together and that between His attributes, there are no contradictions. He works in complete unity of being. Few investments of time and effort are more rewarding for the child of God than contemplating the character of God. To see God for who He is gives us a God-centered perspective of life and ministry.

PSALM 146: TRUST NOT PRINCES, BUT GOD

Theme: God's compassionate faithfulness

Reader Insight: A hallelujah hymn

PSALM SUMMARY

Praise to God! (146:1–2). The first two verses are the psalmist's pledge to "praise the LORD." The word *praise* is emphatic, occurring four times.

Trust not in princes (146:3–4). The psalmist counseled his readers not to put their trust in princes "who cannot save." They are mere "mortal men" (v. 3). When they die, their plans and promises perish with them (v. 4).

Trust in God (146:5–9). "Blessed is he whose help is the God of Jacob" (v. 5). This beatitude gives us the reason for the psalmist's praise. His hope

Psalms 146—150 are known as the "Hallelujah Psalms" because they begin and end with that Hebrew word *hallelujah.* It is a transliteration of the Hebrew word that literally means "praise the Lord." The social emphasis found in this psalm is much like that of the prophets and Jesus.

was in the Lord, who made heaven and earth (v. 6), for God "remains faithful forever" (v. 6). His promises never fail since He is eternal.

The psalmist cited a series of acts of the Almighty to show how He cares about the needs of human beings:

- He "upholds the cause of the oppressed."
- He "gives food to the hungry."
- He "sets prisoners free."
- He "gives sight to the blind."
- He "lifts up those who are bowed down."
- He "watches over the alien" (strangers).
- He "sustains the fatherless and the widow."

What an impressive list of social concerns! The gospel is one, but its application is both personal and social. God helps those who cannot help themselves.

■ *The beatitude in this section gives us the rea-*
■ *son for the psalmist's praise: His hope was in*
■ *the Lord, who made heaven and earth. The*
■ *psalmist listed several of the needs and cares*
■ *of mankind that God addresses.*

Lessons in Living: For the believer, God is more than refuge and shelter. He also strengthens and sustains His own. Join the psalmist's praise for the God of Jacob.

Concluding praise (146:10). God's kingdom and reign will last forever, "to all generations." Hallelujah!

GUIDING QUESTIONS

1. What is the meaning of the term *hallelujah*?
2. What was the reason for the psalmist's praise?
3. The psalmist discussed God's cares about the needs of mankind. What does God do for mankind?

PSALM 147:
THE WINTER PSALM

Background: This hymn praises God for His power and providential care. It appears to be three psalms combined into one.

Theme: God's love and power

Reader Insights: A hallelujah hymn. This hymn alternates between praising God as protector of Israel and as Creator.

PSALM SUMMARY

Great is the Lord who builds up Jerusalem (147:1–6). God is praised for rebuilding Jerusalem after the Babylonian Exile. God is gracious and worthy of our praise (v. 1). He brought the exiles back to Jerusalem, bound up their wounds, and healed them (vv. 2–3). God "sustains the humble" (v. 6).

Jerusalem was overrun by ruthless invaders and its Temple destroyed on three occasions: Solomon's Temple was plundered and burned in 586 B.C.; Zerubbabel's in 20 B.C.; and Herod's in A.D. 70.

God, who numbered and named the stars, created and controls the universe and keeps us by His providential power despite outward circumstances. "Great is our LORD" (v. 5).

- Jerusalem has been overrun three times by
- enemies. In this psalm the people praised
- God for rebuilding Jerusalem after the Baby-
- lonian Exile.

The great sustainer of Creation (147:7–11). The psalmist praised God for His sustaining providence. "He covers the sky with clouds," sends rain, makes the grass grow, feeds both birds and beasts (vv. 8–9). God does not take pleasure in the strength of animals or humans. What pleases Him are people who respond to Him in faith and hope (vv. 10–11).

■ *The psalmist praised God for His sustaining*
■ *providence in maintaining His creation.*

The great God of winter and spring (147:12–20). The psalmist praised God for protecting Jerusalem, blessing her sons, and giving the city peace (v. 13). God also provided them with bread to eat (v. 14).

One almost shivers while reading the psalmist's description of winter. God "spreads the snow like wool" and "scatters the frost like ashes" (v. 16). He covers the land with ice—"Who can stand his icy blast?" (v. 17).

God is also the author of surprising springtime. "He sends his word and melts" the ice, snow, and frost. Warm winds blow and refreshing snow waters flow (v. 18).

God had been especially gracious to Israel, giving them His Word and Law (vv. 19–20).

The poem concludes with a hallelujah! It is important that people be sensitive to God's presence in the world and that this sensitivity evoke their praise.

- *God is the author of the seasons, and it was*
- *He who provided protection for Jerusalem.*
- *God had been especially gracious to Israel,*
- *giving them His Word and the Law.*

Lessons in Living: God's creative work is not limited to our physical world. He is also doing a creative work in the lives of Christians. Submit to Him and allow Him to build and sustain your life.

GUIDING QUESTIONS

1. What are the key thoughts of this psalm?
2. God is the Creator and sustainer of His creation. What do those truths mean to us?
3. What picture did the psalmist paint of God?

PSALM 148: A CALL TO UNIVERSAL PRAISE

Background: The occasion for this psalm is indicated in the closing verse, which is an allusion to Israel's return after the Exile.

Theme: All creation praises God.

Reader Insights: A hallelujah hymn. This psalm is a celebration of God as Creator of everything from angels (v. 2) to insects (v. 10). It is actually a series of calls to worship. It has been the inspiration of many Christian hymns, including Francis of Assisi's "All Creatures of Our God and King." Those who trust in the Lord need have no fear of nature.

PSALM SUMMARY

Praise in heaven (148:1–6). The psalmist called on all celestial creatures to praise the Lord because He made them and sustains them (see Jer. 31:35–36). Those listed in the psalm include: "all his angels, . . . all his heavenly hosts . . . sun and moon, . . . all you shining stars." Highest heaven and the waters above the heavens (the source of rain) are invited to praise

God. God created them, established them, and controls them (vv. 5–6).

- *The psalmist called on all celestial creatures*
- *to praise the Lord because He made the heav-*
- *ens and sustains them.*

Praise on earth (148:7–14). Next, the psalmist summoned all earthly creatures to praise God. He cited the monsters of the sea, "lightning and hail, snow and clouds, stormy winds"—all forces of nature. God is to be praised by everything from above the heavens to everything beneath the sea. These include "mountains and all hills, fruit trees and all cedars, wild animals and all cattle," creeping insects, and soaring birds (vv. 9–10).

The Lord's name is to be exalted, and His glory will fill heaven and earth (v. 13). "He has raised up for his people a horn" (v. 14) is a reference to God's restoration of Israel's honor after the humiliation of the Babylonian captivity.

Kings and common people are called on to praise God. Young men, young women, old people, and children were invited to join "all his saints" (the devout) in praise (vv. 11–12, 14).

Lessons in Living: All creation praises God, for all of creation was created by Him through His creative word. But God not only commands His creation; He also sustains it. In the New Testament, the name to which all creation is related is Jesus Christ. The One who sustains the universe is also Lord of the believer's life. What a great encouragement for the believer!

"Praise the LORD" (v. 14b). God's creation and providence constitute both a call to praise and a summons to service on the part of His people. The praise of God is an obligation as well as a privilege and a joy. It is at the heart of Christian service.

- *The psalmist summoned all earthly creatures*
- *to praise God. His name is to be exalted, and*
- *His glory will fill heaven and earth.*

GUIDING QUESTIONS

1. What was the occasion of this outburst of praise for God?

2. From what sectors did the psalmist summon praise?

3. How does this call to praise God apply to believers today?

PSALM 149: A SONG OF VICTORY

- - - -

Theme: God's rule allows no rival—whether enemies, evil, or death.

Reader Insights: A hallelujah hymn

PSALM SUMMARY

Israel's victory over her enemies (149:1–4). These introductory verses are an invitation to praise God. In verse 1 the psalmist called on the people to "praise the LORD" and to "sing to the LORD a new song" (see Pss. 33:3; 96:1). This is an expression of gratitude to God for a military victory. The people praised God with a sacred dance while making melody with the tambourine (timbrel) and harp (lyre).

The psalmist then added the assurance that God takes delight in His people and rewards their humility with salvation.

- As an expression of gratitude for a military
- victory, the psalmist called on the people to
- "praise the LORD" and to "sing to the LORD a
- new song."

Background: This vigorous psalm of praise is a kind of war dance. "The nations revolt against the rule of God over all the world as it is revealed on Zion (cf. Pss. 2:1f; 9:19) . . . The kings of the [heathen] nations revolt against Yahweh (cf. Pss. 2:2, 10; 48:4). Both traditions echo in Psalm 149" (Hans-Joachim Kraus, *Psalms 60–150*, trans. Hilton C. Oswald [Minneapolis: Fortress Press, 1993], 566–67).

We also find a New Testament correlation with this passage in John 16:11. In view of Christ's work on the cross, "this is the judgment written by the cross against the 'ruler of this world' (John 16:11), who is the power behind the kings of verse 8" (Derek Kidner, *Psalms 73–150* [Downers Grove, Ill.: Inter-Varsity Press, 1975], 490).

God's judgment on Israel's enemies (149:5–9). The faithful people of God exulted in the glory of their triumph and sang for joy (v. 5). They praise God with their voices and a sword dance (v. 6). The sword the psalmist refers to was double-edged, designed to cut two ways. Israel's victory represented vengeance, chastisement, and the execution of God's judgment on their enemies (vv. 7–9). Here we see the notion that Israel considered her enemies to be God's enemies.

The execution of God's judgment is the "sentence written" in verse 9. This judgment is "written at the core of biblical revelation (see Deut. 30:15–19). The absolute and irrevocable judgment of God rests upon *all* nations, even including Israel, God's chosen people" (George A. F. Knight, *Psalms*, vol. 2 [Philadelphia: Westminster, 1983], 364).

God's Judgment on Israel's Enemies

Lessons in Living: God allows us a range of experiences so that we may learn new and deeper dimensions of His love and grace. Just like Israel, we also face difficult situations. From Eph. 6:10–18, we learn that spiritual conflict requires spiritual weapons. The joyful praise of God's people is the weapon by which they conquer all their enemies.

FORM OF JUDGMENT	PASSAGE	DESCRIPTION
Vengeance	v. 7	"to inflict vengeance on the nations and punishment on the peoples"
Chastisement	v. 8.	"to bind their kings with fetters, their nobles with shackles of iron"
Sentencing	v. 9	"to carry out the sentence written against them"

- Israel exulted in the glory of their triumph
- and sang for joy. Their victory represented
- vengeance, chastisement, and the execution
- of God's judgment on their enemies.

GUIDING QUESTIONS

1. What was this psalm's background?

2. Why were the people of Israel praising God?

3. Describe God's judgment on Israel's enemies. What are the future implications of God's judgment?

4. What personal lessons for living the life of faith do we learn from this psalm of victory?

PSALM 150: A DOXOLOGY OF PRAISE

Theme: Praise to God

Reader Insights: A hallelujah hymn. This festive hymn of praise is a fitting climax to the Psalms. It is a doxology that reaches a crescendo of voices and instruments. The loud, joyful, and exultant tone of the psalm tells us something of the nature of Israel's worship. It could be solemn and grand without tedium or empty pomp. In these six verses the psalmist answered four questions: where, why, how, and by whom God is to be praised.

PSALM SUMMARY

Where do we praise God? (150:1). The Lord is to be praised "in his sanctuary," the Temple in

"Praise Him"

This phrase appears ten times in the six verses of this psalm. The first occurrence identifies "Him" as God, "the Power directing the universe and all it contains" (A. Cohen, ed., *The Psalms* [New York: Soncino Press, 1974], 479).

"Music provides the singing with a special power which is appropriate for the majestic greatness of the God of Israel. But all singing and music making is directed to Yahweh by means of the tenfold repeated 'praise Him'; it points to his exalted person. By that the magic of that which is musical is broken through" (Hans-Joachim Kraus, *Psalms 60–150*, trans. [Minneapolis: Fortress Press, 1993], 571).

We find a contrast to this psalm in the teachings of Jesus, "My kingdom is not of this world" (John 18:36). Paul taught that our warfare and weapons are not human but spiritual, to be used against evil (see 2 Cor. 10:3–4). Seen in the context of its times, this psalm is understandable. The unfortunate truth is that we, as God's people, seem to make so little progress in learning to love our enemies and make them our friends. All too often we seek vengeance, claiming that God is always on our side, despite the teachings of our Lord.

Lessons in Living: How do you praise God? Do you praise Him for the right reasons? Take time to contemplate His mighty deeds, for they reveal His mighty character. Then join with all creation in praising God.

Jerusalem. Also, His glory is to be sung in the world He has created.

Why do we praise God? (150:2). He is due honor "for his mighty deeds" on behalf of His people. He deserves our praise also because of His wonderful character, which is revealed in nature as well as His actions.

How are we to praise God? (150:3–5). Here we have the most extensive list of musical instruments in the Old Testament. God was to be praised "with the sounding of the trumpet." The biblical trumpet was not a horn made of metal but a ram's horn.

The lute and harp or lyre were stringed instruments. A timbrel was a small drum similar to a tambourine. Pipes were probably reed flutes. "Resounding cymbals" were also used along with dance in praise of God.

Who is to praise God? (150:6). The poem reaches its climax as the psalmist sang, "Let everything that has breath praise the LORD!" Hallelujah! All creatures including mankind are meant to glorify God, who made and sustains them.

This is a psalm of pure ecstatic praise. The words *breath* and *spirit* are the same word in Hebrew, Greek, and Latin. God gives us life (breath) and renews our spirits so we may praise Him. Praise begins and ends with God. Human sin and forgetfulness violate the purpose for which He made us.

The Psalter could not come to a more appropriate close than with Psalm 150. It is a pinnacle of praise in the Old Testament hymnbook of praises. It celebrates God's presence in His world and among His people.

GUIDING QUESTIONS

1. Describe the scene that the psalmist conveyed to his readers.

2. The psalmist answered four questions: where, why, how, and by whom God is to be praised. What were his answers to these questions?

3. What is the climax of this poem? How does the Psalter close?

CHRIST IN THE PSALMS

One of the most controversial questions facing interpreters of the book of Psalms is how to understand the many references to the "king" or "anointed one" (Hebrew *Messiah*). Do these references speak of a human king of ancient Israel or point ahead to Jesus as the ideal King and Messiah?

The biblical writers wrote of real-life persons and situations. The king played a most prominent role in ancient Israel's national life. More than sixty references in the Psalms highlight the king's prestige. The original readers of the Psalms naturally understood that these references spoke of the human king, whose role was so very important in their day-to-day existence. Because the basic meaning of any text is what the author intended the original audience to understand, "king" in the Psalms refers primarily to a human king of ancient Israel.

It may be possible for references to the "king" or "anointed one" to speak of both a human king and point ahead to Jesus as the ideal One.

The only clear passage that describes a human king in its Old Testament context who is seen as the ideal messianic King in a subsequent text is Psalm 2 (Heb. 1:5 treats this psalm as explicitly messianic). Thus, the human king in Psalm 2 functioned as a type, that is, one who had significance in his own historical setting but who also served as a divinely ordained foreshadowing of someone in later biblical revelation.

Generally speaking, references to the king in Psalms speak of the human king in the biblical writer's time. Occasionally, reference to the king was originally understood as a human king but later applied to the ideal Messiah. In one psalm (Ps. 110) the king can mean none other than the ideal messianic King of kings.

The superscription of Psalm 110 portrays it as Davidic. Surprisingly, the first verse speaks of David's successor as his lord. In ancient Israel this was inconceivable. David was the greatest king, the standard by which his successors were measured. Early in Israel's history this passage was understood as a prophecy of the coming Messiah. Jesus interpreted Psalm 110:1 in this way in a dispute with the Pharisees (Matt. 22:41–55; Mark 12:35–37; Luke 20:41–44). Jesus' riddle—if "David himself calls him 'Lord,' how then can he be his son?"—captures the mystery of the incarnation. Jesus is the Son of David but also more than David's son (Rom. 1:3–4).

(Taken from *Holman Bible Handbook*, p. 340.)

VENGEANCE AND VINDICATION

Sensitive readers of the Psalms have long been troubled by the harsh expression of vengeance uttered by psalmists, often attributed to David himself. Take for example these statements:

• "Break the arm of the wicked and evil man: call him to account for his wickedness" (Ps. 10:15);

• "Let the wicked be put to shame and lie silent in the grave" (Ps. 31:17); and

• "The righteous will be glad when they are avenged, when they bathe their feet in the blood of the wicked" (Ps. 58:6–10).

Such unloving statements raise serious ethical questions about the vindictive spirit reflected in these statements. Other prominent curses are found in Psalms 3:7; 5:10; 28:4; 35; 40:14–15; 55; 69; 79; 109; 137; 139:19–22; 140:9–10. Attempts to explain such fierce expressions fall into several categories.

First, some think that these curses only reflect the humanity of the author expressing his deepest desires for vindication when wronged by the wicked.

Thus, he was reflecting a lower standard of morality than that found in the New Testament. This explanation does not adequately account for the fact that the verses in which these curses occur are inspired by the very God who taught the virtue of turning the other cheek.

We must also recognize that 1 Samuel portrays David in a very different light. Although provoked almost beyond imagination, David did not respond vengefully but by tolerance and patience. The occasions on which David refused to kill his mortal enemy Saul provide eloquent testimony to this. Furthermore, Leviticus 19:18 forbids any attempt to exact vengeance against personal enemies, arguing against interpreting these curses as personal vendettas.

Second, another explanation sees the curses as only predictions of the enemy's ruin rather than as expressions of the psalmist's desire that the enemy meet an unhappy end. But Psalm 59 is clearly a prayer to God in which the psalmist asks God to wreak havoc on his enemies.

A plausible understanding of these difficult sayings must take account of the significant role enemies play in the book of Psalms. Their presence goes far beyond the relatively limited number of psalms that curse the psalmist's enemies. The psalmists were often kings or represented the king in some official capacity. God mandated Israel's king to rule over God's covenant people in order to safeguard them and all God had promised to do through them.

Thus, any threat to God's people was also a threat to the very promise of God. In this unique situation, to oppose the God-anointed king was to oppose God Himself. So the king/psalmist prayed that God would judge those evildoers who intended to hinder the work of God, desiring that God and His work on earth would be vindicated.

Because of the unique position held by the king as God's anointed, he represented God's will in a measure unlike that of anyone today. For this reason believers today must not pray curses, for they are not in a position like that of the king/psalmist in ancient Israel.

(Taken from *Holman Bible Handbook*, p. 335.)

The following list is a collection of the sources used for this volume. All are from Broadman & Holman's list of published reference resources. They accommodate the reader's need for more specific information and/or for an expanded treatment of *Psalms,* vol. 3. These works will greatly aid in the reader's study, teaching, and presentation of the Psalms. The accompanying annotations can be helpful in guiding the reader to the proper resources.

Cate, Robert L. *An Introduction to the Old Testament and Its Study.* A scholarly treatment of Old Testament issues and topics. The author deals with history and various schools of thought. He presents his material in such a way that the reader can grasp the content of the Old Testament and come to view it as a book of faith.

Holman Bible Dictionary. An exhaustive, alphabetically arranged resource of Bible-related subjects. An excellent tool of definitions and other information on the people, places, things, and events of the Bible.

Holman Bible Handbook, pp. 323–50. A comprehensive treatment that offers outlines, commentary on key themes and sections, and full-color photos, illustrations, charts, and maps. Provides an accent on the broader theological teachings.

Holman Book of Biblical Charts, Maps, and Reconstructions. A colorful, visual collection of charts, maps, and reconstructions, These well-designed tools are invaluable to the study of the Bible.

McEachern, Alton H. *Psalms* (Layman's Bible Book Commentary, vol. 8). A popular-level treatment of the Psalms. This easy-to-use volume provides a relevant and practical perspective for the reader. *Shepherd's Notes—Psalms 101–150* has drawn heavily on many of the outlines from Dr. McEachern's volume.

McQuay, Earl P. *Keys to Interpreting the Bible.* This work provides a fine introduction to the study of the Bible that is invaluable for home Bible studies, lay members of a local church, or students.

SHEPHERD'S NOTES

SHEPHERD'S NOTES

SHEPHERD'S NOTES

SHEPHERD'S NOTES

SHEPHERD'S NOTES